The Cycle to Hampden

To every person that contributed to this book. To every person that helped my dream of keeping my Granda's memory alive become a tangible eternity. I thank you.

The Cycle to Hampden

The story of Joseph McGunnigle and his lifelong dedication to Scottish football.

By Cassie McGunnigle

Contents

Foreword by Neil Drysdale

It doesn't happen very often that you meet somebody with such infinite joie de vivre and positivity that they are capable of elevating your spirits in the space of a few minutes.

And I was not expecting my visit to Joe McGunnigle's home in 2018 to be a bundle of laughs, considering the fact he had been diagnosed with stage four head and neck cancer two years earlier.

As a feature writer with the Press and Journal, I was covering the 'Courage on the Catwalk' and 'BRAVE' charity initiatives to help raise money for Friends of Anchor; events which have allowed scores of people, male and female, to strut their stuff at Aberdeen's famous Art Deco, Beach Ballroom.

In one sense, these meetings with the models, of all ages and backgrounds, offered the chance to highlight the strength of the human spirit and explain how the catwalk shows provided an escape from the often-harsh reality of gruelling chemotherapy sessions involved in tackling an illness that affects almost every family.

When facing a cancer diagnosis, it can prove more than difficult to remain upbeat. Families become familiar with a solemn atmosphere. The tristesse in their stories cast a cloud. Laughs are in short supply. It can be so challenging to keep a light mood when there is a dark shadow hanging over the landscape.

And then there was Joe. A man with a capacity for finding silver linings in every situation, a redoubtable Aberdonian with a sense of the absurd and a tangible determination to prove that, even if the end was in sight, he was going to enjoy the journey, prove it was a wonderful life, and keep on fighting to the end of the road.

This blithe man was such a breath of fresh air on our initial tryst. His vocal cords had been ravaged to the stage where the conversation was initially difficult. But then, bit by bit, I was enthralled by the McGunnigle magic, and we talked about his decades of following the Scotland football team across the globe to more than 50 different countries.

He was in his pomp while his beloved compatriots qualified for World Cups regularly from the 1970s to the 1990s. And he travelled to Germany, Spain, Mexico, France... Wherever there was the opportunity to cheer on different teams, from the days of Kenny Dalglish and Denis Law, to John Collins and the rest of the tartan warriors who tackled Brazil in the opening match of the 1998 World Cup in France.

Joe wasn't a parochial supporter. On the contrary, he relished meeting fans from other countries, and they rejoiced in his company. He was famous for collecting memorabilia from all those far-flung places, but he also made sure his hosts in Europe and further afield enjoyed the best Scottish hospitality.

His granddaughter Cassie has done a marvelous job in collating so many cherished moments from his peripatetic life. But then again, Joe was one of those rare people who could forge a bond with strangers and make them feel special.

Even during that first meeting, he kept turning adversity to advantage. He derived delight from his last meal – before important surgery – at the Ashvale chipper in Aberdeen. Then he told me about how his reaction to learning he had a rare cancer was to say: "Well, I'm a rare specimen myself". And, as he spoke, I still remember the sound of laughter reverberating through his house.

Just a few months later, he was one of the star attractions at the BRAVE shows where he sashayed onto the catwalk as if he had been taking lessons from Twiggy and looked as if it was his natural milieu.

Behind the scenes, his daughter, Karen, was worried that the demands of the event might prove too much for her beloved dad – and she was right to have concerns. Joe had not long finished another round of chemotherapy one week before the show.

These shows can be uplifting for the participants and the audience members, and they have raised more than a million pounds for Friends of Anchor since they started in 2013. But they can also test the mettle and endurance of those who take part, all of whom have been affected by cancer. Yet, while finalising his preparations for taking centre stage, with a smile which brought the house down, Joe gave me the thumbs up and told me it would be sensational – and he was right.

He may have died at the start of 2020, but the myriad memories, anecdotes, and recollections of those who knew him paint a glorious picture of a man with an insatiable exuberance, a force of nature, somebody who loved football - and who was a very efficient coach and official in the northeast, even though he didn't toot his own horn.

But above all, he was devoted to those close to him and the smile on his face when he was photographed at Aberdeen Beach with his beautiful little dog, Misty, by my colleague Colin Rennie, is one of those images which sticks in the mind. It struck a chord with everybody who saw it. Even now, I seem to have some grit in my eye when I look back on it.

But enough. Joe McGunnigle wouldn't have wanted anybody to indulge in sentimental nonsense or fret over his illness. He was one of those indomitable souls who might have died but who has never really left us.

And this book amply illustrates that he was one in a million — a man with an all-consuming zest for life right to the end.

I feel very privileged to have met him and his family. But now, let's cry "Action" on these magical McGunnigle memoirs!

Preface

If you were to ask me what my greatest attribute is, I would say my understanding of love: a trait that I inherited from my beloved grandparents, who raised me. The unconditional love that I received and, in return, was able to give has made me the person I am today. Things are never as bad as they can be if you have love, no matter the storm.

I lost my beautiful Nana after only eleven years. She shared a love with me that was invincible. Her love was warm and nurturing. I remember how she used to squeeze into my single bed to hold me, even in her final months. She made me feel like nothing in this world could ever hurt me. I can still feel it.

I lost the first man I ever loved after only twenty-three years, my Granda. For 23 incredible years, I witnessed his strength, bravery, and wisdom. When my Nana died when I was aged eleven, it seemed that coming out the other end was near impossible. My Granda raised me through my teenage years into adulthood and I owe every ounce of who I am today to him. He shaped the way I look at the world.

I count my blessings every day to have had those special years with you both. And although I miss you every moment of every day, I would allow that pain again, and again, because it is a small price to pay for such love.

My Granda was many things to me. He was the first man I ever loved; he was the man that would teach me right from wrong. He was the man who encouraged me to be the best version of myself and achieve great things. He was the man that would teach me to be fair to others. He was the man that could have won every episode of 'Who Wants to be a Millionaire'. He was the international Tartan Army foot soldier that was adored by many. He was the manager of an amateur football team on a Saturday afternoon. He was the owner of a wicked sense of humour and a sharp tongue. He was a wonderful singer. He was a brilliant narrator.

He was the man that made me never want to go to sleep because his storytelling was so enthralling. He was the man who held my hand and hugged me when I cried. He was the man that kept us afloat after we lost Nana. He was the man who loved his family more than anything in the world. And amongst all of those, he was my Granda.

This book is to ensure that there is a lasting memory of that man. This book is for me. This book is for you. This book is for everyone who Joe McGunnigle touched. Granda, you continue to inspire me in every way, even though you are no longer here. I might not see you anymore, but I can always hear you and know exactly what you would tell me next.

You were a gift to us all, and you have changed the way we see life for the better. Even when tomorrow was not always easy to face, you got up, put on your nicest trousers, your pressed shirt and your funky hat, and you made us laugh, you made us cry, and you showed us that tomorrow is nothing to be scared of when you have today.

"As for dying? I'll haud gaun." - Joe McGunnigle, 04/03/2019

Introduction

The best thing about having a passion in life is how unique they can be to us. We all care about things differently, some of us more than others. Sharing a passion creates a unity that no other shared thing can provide. We share cake, a pie, a conversation and, even more likely, a few bottles of whisky, but none of these compare to what a shared passion gives to like-minded individuals. There was a man who had a lot of passion and there was nothing he loved more than to share it with others. That passion was following Scotland, and he had just about enough of it to become one of the greatest Scottish football supporters of all time. His name was Joseph Docherty McGunnigle: known and loved by many of you as Joe. The man I hold the privilege to call Granda.

The wise words of Thomas Dexter Jakes say:

"If you can't figure out your purpose, figure out your passion. For your passion will lead you right into your purpose."

My Granda was here to be known, to be loved, and to inspire. In following Scotland worldwide for sixty years, he fulfilled each of those, and in this, I know he found his purpose.

Hindsight is the funniest of things. Without my Granda's love of following Scotland, he would not have lived the life he did, met the people he had, or left an imprint on the lives of so many. Having a passion can open one door and unlock a thousand others.

But be careful to assume passion as only a pastime or hobby. For passion comes from the heart. And you've got to follow your heart – it should be an obligation. I will always remember my Granda by these nine moving words he would say to my Nana in response to her humorous grumbling:

"Following Scotland is not a holiday, Cath. It's duty!"

Chapter 1: The Cycle to Hampden

Born in Aberdeen on 20th November 1942, Joseph Doherty McGunnigle was the youngest child to Thomas and Williamina (Minnie) McGunnigle. He was brother to Thomas (Tommy), Patrick (Pat), Frank (Francis) and Catherine (Cath). Not too far from the railway line that runs

Granda as a bairn

Granda with his Mum and Dad

through Woodside, they lived in a basic house, known as No.9 Ferrier Gardens. Thomas worked as a labourer and in various other jobs like such, and Minnie worked at Richard's on Marmalade Street as a weaver, after an early career in the fish industry.

In the early days of my Granda's life, his elder brothers Pat and Tommy worked away in the Navy. They were a modest family that did not have much. His brothers did all they could to support their family. Granda's Mum and Dad had both died at a young age, and this left the siblings with the

Frank, Cathy, Granda and Tommy

responsibility to care for and look after one another by whatever means necessary.

'When our mum got ill, Joe, Cathy and I were sent out to Linn Moor Children's Home to be looked after. Our brother Tommy was working at the time, so he couldn't take care of us. Joe and I had quite enough of Linn Moor, so we escaped out the window and left Cathy behind. When Tommy found us at home the next *day, he was furious that we had left her and went back to pick her up. We didn't ever go back. Tommy made it work.'*

Granda attended St. Peter's primary school on Nelson Street. He was inquisitive from a young age and always keen to read and learn. Because of this, he had the opportunity to attend the prestigious Robert Gordon's School with a scholarship, but the family could not afford basic things such as books and uniforms, so he did not go.

His inquisitiveness extended to the world around him too. As a young boy, Granda spent a lot of time outdoors. He loved adventuring and making the most of the surrounding natural resources. He swam in the River Don during the summer and went ice skating over frozen ponds in winter months. He also enjoyed watching the local blacksmith make horseshoes and paid careful attention to his craft.

'We were brought up in Woodside. We didn't have much, but we weren't aware of what we didn't have. We used to collect buckies and sell them for a penny a

cup. We would go round Ferrier gardens selling them... I think that's where some salesmanship instincts started for Joe!'

Although there was not much in the way of money, there was companionship. Woodside was the place where Granda met many of his lifelong friends, including Micky McDonald, Sandy Robertson, Allan Black (Blackie) and lastly, the love of his life, my beloved Nana, Cath.

Granda and the love of his life, my Nana

'Life was so different then. We didn't have much in the way of material things, but we had each other. We laughed a lot. The good and the bad, I wouldn't change any of it.'

My Nana was born on Hayton Road, Tillydrone, which was a short walk from Ferrier Gardens. She was working as a Bakery assistant when she first met Granda but soon after re-trained as a fish filleter, where she more or less remained for the rest of her working life. She was known to be a highly regarded, fast and skilled worker.

My Nana and Granda met in their local neighbourhood of Woodside in 1962, when Granda was 19 and Nana was 17. Granda suggested a first date at the pictures but on the day, he had no money, so a walk round the River Don was the start of their lifelong romance. They were married by Father Butler at St. Joseph's RC Church after a two-year courtship and engagement, followed by a wedding reception for family and friends at the Embassy Rooms in Woodside.

Granda had developed a love for animals at a young age, and this never left him as a married man. It was obvious, from the time as a young boy when he would catch tadpoles breed them into frogs to keep, to some of the stranger pets he cared for over the years, that his fascination and love for them was universal. Sometimes, to the surprise of those around him.

'One day, I came home from work and there was a strange noise coming from underneath Joe's bed. I

think it was a hiss. I put my hand underneath to feel about, and something sunk its teeth right into my hand. It was a polecat! He had snuck a polecat home and under his bed. Don't ask where he got it from.'

Suffice to say, the polecat wasn't a long-lasting pet in the McGunnigle household, but it was just the beginning of a succession of animal companions for Granda. He mostly had dogs, but one furry friend in particular raised a lot of eyebrows. Snowy, Granda's pet rabbit, used to accompany him every day while he worked at Aberdeen Airport. Granda would let Snowy sit in the front seat of his car and then whilst he worked all day, the white ball of fur would run around the outdoor grounds of the airport and through the runways, always returning to him at the end of the day.

Granda enjoyed his career as an aircraft fitter/engineer at Aberdeen Airport. He was employed there for most of his working life, growing into the position after a variety of manual jobs as a young adult. At 16-years old he was seafaring in a trawler, but his final job was on solid land, where he founded and ran his own business, Premier Kitchens. He took great pride in supplying and coordinating the fitting of kitchens for friends and family.

Granda was not strictly qualified to be an aircraft engineer but he somehow managed to slide into the realm – an opportunity that wouldn't exist today. Granda's job at the airport was a step upward for the family and it meant better things for the house and nicer holidays too. He worked at the airport for almost twenty years before venturing off down the path of kitchen design. I was lucky to speak with Richard Towns, who worked alongside Granda at Aberdeen Airport.

'How do I begin to tell you about Joe's life as an Aircraft Engineer? I'll assume that you know next to nothing about the airline, its people, the workings of the airport and what we did. British Air Ferries was a small airline based in Southend. Aberdeen was an outstation operating only two aircraft. One aircraft was to do all the flying and the other one was a spare. We needed two because they were old and constantly breaking down. Our primary mission was to get Shell oil rig workers up to Sumburgh and back four times a

day and during my last summer there, weekend flights to the Channel Islands.

British Air Ferries was a cheap airline and as such, all our equipment was old. Everything we owned often broke down, but worst of all, we had no hangar space. We carried out our work outside and this was challenging when it was dark, or the weather was terrible. One memory that still haunts me is when we changed a component held together by only two nuts and bolts and an electrical connection. We were buried arm deep in the ice-cold engine with a gale-force wind blasting us with almost freezing sleet in the wee hours of the morning. That half-hour job took over three hours.

Most of our team were English and Joe was very Scottish. It was quaint to hear him speak slowly and "properly" to the English members of the team. I am a boy from Woodside and went to Powis School, so I also found it funny watching the English listen to Joe.

The airport social life was pretty good. All the airlines

were small and there were a lot of parties and friendships. I can't remember how Joe became an Aircraft Engineer. I think he may have known someone who got him a job helping with the vehicles and ground equipment and then fell into working on the aircraft. In Engineering, we had only five people; the boss and two teams. Joe and I were the "A Team" and you can guess who called us that. The other team didn't have a name. Joe and I would do a couple of weeks of day shift and then a couple of weeks of nights. We did it together for three and a half years, and Joe was there for a couple of years after I left.

Each shift had both advantages and disadvantages. The day shift had to get to the airport in time to prepare and launch the aircraft for the first flight of the day, which we began by connecting an external diesel power set to the plane and flicking a few switches on the flight deck to get the lights on and some other things working. By then, we'd know how many gallons of fuel the pilot wanted and had to work out how much to put in each of the four tanks, convert that into litres and let the man from Shell pump it in.

When all was done, we'd sit on the aircraft and chat with the hostesses until the passengers arrived. The aircraft would return two and a half hours later, and then we would do it all again. By the time the aircraft was back for the third rotation of the day, the other shift had arrived, and if the aircraft were good to go, we would go home.

If we were on the late shift, we would do what was necessary to get rid of the aircraft and then continue doing anything that had to be done to the spare or work on the ground equipment. If there was nothing to do, we would do just that. I read a lot of books at work. When the aircraft returned from its last flight, we would debrief the pilot and discover what they had broken that day. There was nearly always something.

I have given you a background into what we did at work, so I'll now talk about my friend Joe, your most excellent Granda. Joe and I had very little in common. As I type, I'm trying to think of anything we had in common before we met. Politics was a big one. We were both Socialists, me probably more to the left than Joe. We once went to vote for the SNP together. I lived near the Logie end of Provost Rust Drive, so we had the same polling station.

Joe was a man who always knew a man. He was a man who could get things. He had been working at the airport for a long time and was known as quite a character, which there's no denying that he was. Joe didn't mind a bit of mischief. His spirit and enthusiasm were something to behold. I have tears in my eyes and a lump in my throat as I type. Joe was one in a million.'

Granda liked to keep himself busy. In between Scotland games and a hectic work schedule, he got involved with local politics. He grew up maturing an interest in the SNP and from a young age he was a keen supporter and participated in canvassing and local counselling. He frequently attended rallies and leafleted all around the city. He never lost hope in the possibility of a better future for young people in Scotland and believed in equal opportunities for all.

The thing about Granda is that he didn't just laze about and expect change to happen. He acted on it. He always voiced his beliefs, without being disrespectful. He had a constant reserve of energy to fight the status quo and never let cynicism hold him back from communicating this. Granda didn't let his friends get lost amongst this either, he always tried to get better opportunities for people, such as connecting them with others that could help better their position or bringing them along with him to work.

'Being brought up in Woodside, I think Joe saw a lot that shouldn't have happened. We had to do so many things just to get bus fare. He always stood up for what was right. I suppose that's why he got so involved with local politics. He didn't like an injustice.'

Granda wanted to see positive change happen and for life to be better for those with limited opportunities in Scotland. He always saw the greatest potential of his country and its people.

He was an incredibly patriotic man and a firm believer in Scottish independence being the answer to many of the limitations in Scotland. A patriot, a nationalist, an advocate for Scottish freedom. If you just add die-hard

Tartan Army supporter into the personality equation, you've got a wee bit of Joe.

Chapter 2: Say goodbye to Saturdays for the rest of your life!

Before I delve more into what this book is really about, I think it's best to tell you a bit about my Granda's involvement with amateur football, the Aberdeenshire Amateur Football Association (A.A.F.A), the Scottish Amateur Football Association (S.A.F.A) and some of the adventures that came with it. Granda dedicated a large portion of his thinking time to planning Scotland trips but spent an equal amount trying to solve problems related to amateur football.

He was the manager of what was formerly known as Waterton Thistle F.C and now known as Woodside Amateur Football Club. Waterton Thistle was formed in 1963 and Granda was involved with them since they established him as the secretary for the first ten years. He became the manager in 1974 and enforced the transition to re-naming the team to Woodside in 1991, to coincide with the 100th anniversary of Woodside District becoming a Royal Burgh (Woodside... A royal burgh. Who would have known?). Woodside Amateur F.C. was born. The dynamic of amateur football in Aberdeen was about to change forever. Okay, well, it didn't change overnight, but it was coming!

Granda was adored by his team, no matter how many rotations there were, and new players came and went. I do not doubt that there were quarrels but, overall, he gave so much to the boys he worked alongside. It was often the case that Granda would manage the guys

Granda (far left) with his Waterton Thistle boys.
5th September 1981

throughout their life too. Some had been playing for him since age eighteen and were still playing for him when they were in their thirties and married with children. It wasn't just on the pitch Granda was a manager: he mentored them off the pitch too. He had a unique bond with each and every one of his players and cared about them so much as individuals.

Granda even organised a week-long club tour in Portugal for his beloved Woodside. The very same time that Scotland were due to be in Lisbon for a World Cup tie. Coincidence? I think not. It wouldn't be the first time that Granda conveniently organised a trip around the exact date and location of a Scotland game!

'I didn't want to miss the Scotland match – or Woodside playing. So, I decided it would be best to take the team to Portugal to play a couple of games as well.

I plan to write to Andy Roxburgh (Scotland Manager at the time) and tell him if he doesn't come and support us in our game, then we might decide to stay away from his!'

Now let's be honest, I'm sure there would be no keeping you away from a Scotland game Joe, but a nice bargaining tool indeed!

The boys he took away were so pleased that they had been given this opportunity and vowed to work extra hard to ensure they could get back into Division I, after a rocky previous year of being knocked down into Division V. Long serving player Chris Elliot said at the time:

'We have taken a few drubbings in recently and it would have been easy for Joe to pack us in, but he stuck by us and worked really hard to make sure the club kept going.

He now has the rare luxury of a reasonably sized pool of players to work with. That's because newcomers have found Joe's enthusiasm for Woodside infectious. He would do anything for us. It's time he got something in return.'

Throughout the years, Granda brought Woodside through the ranks. They became a roaring success. Woodside became the team that everybody wanted to be part of. They were a great team with an even greater manager.

Acquiring the nickname "Mr. Woodside" in the process, he led Woodside through triumphant victories and claimed many trophies and titles for Woodside; including four Premier League Titles, Stephen Shield, Division

Granda proud as punch, after the Woodside loons won the Premier League for three consecutive years

One, White Cup, Aberdeen F.C. trophy, John Todd Memorial Trophy, Frank Waugh Shield, North of Scotland Trophy and North of Scotland Cup, to name a few.

Not only did Granda present Woodside as an appealing and successful team for people to join, but it also seemed to appeal to a certain Woodside born, Mr.

Denis Law. Well, according to Granda, Denis was ever so eager to be part of Woodside and it was at his request to become the honorary president but as per this letter and newspaper article, I think we will find it was Granda who asked Denis.

The letter reads:

'Dear Joe,
Thank you for your letter, sorry for taking so long in replying but I have been very busy.

I would be honoured to be your honorary president, thank you very much.

Yours aye,
Denis Law.

17/11/91

Dear Joe,
thank you for your letter, sorry for taking so long in replying but I have been very busy. I will be honoured to be your honary president thank you very much.

Yours aye
Denis Law

P.S.
Thanks for the Woodside Magazine it brought back many memories.

P.s,
thanks for the Woodside magazine, it brought back many memories.'

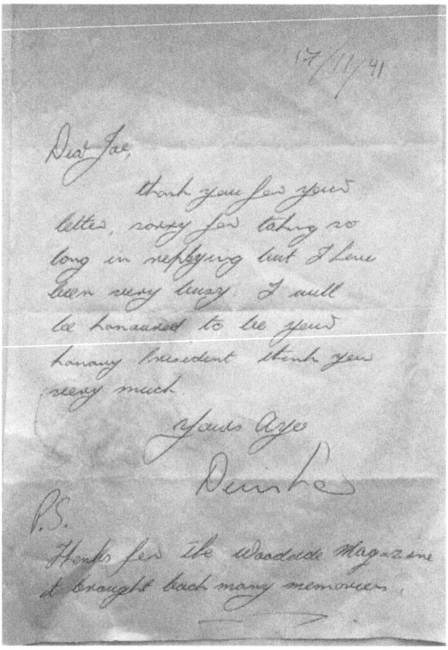

A very kind gesture from Denis, which Granda still spoke of in recent years. Of course, when Denis agreed to become Woodside's honorary president, it was the perfect opportunity for a press release. After all, Granda had the evening express on speed dial by this point. December 1991, lo and behold **"Denis joins Side!"**

So, there you have it, the Woodside area's greatest footballing son accepted an invitation to join Woodside A.F.C. Granda proclaimed in a statement to the Green Final newspaper:

'We are delighted that Denis has agreed to back us in our quest to give the Woodside area a team to be proud of. Hopefully, with Denis as a backer, we can start to build something  *great at amateur level. I have fond memories of seeing Denis Law play for Scotland against Ziare in the 1974 World Cup.'*

But if you think amateur football is all about playing on green grass and reputable honorary presidents, then I am afraid to tell you that you are wrong. There are the away days, the buses home, the on-pitch fights, or "negotiations" rather. The commiserations, the hardcore celebrations and all the antics that come with them! And Granda was involved in them all!

'Your Granda could go anywhere, in any environment. We were playing against Maryculter in a final. Your Granda was the manager of us – Waterton Thistle. It was half-time and we were all getting an orange to eat. I looked over to the opposing side, and I could see a V.I.P marquee. I turned my head slightly and I could see your Granda and Blackie (Alan Black) dancing aboot in it. They were absolutely pished!

I'm standing here wondering, "How the fuck did they get in there and why the fuck are they with the opposing side?"

The marquee was filled with oil tycoons and the local dignitaries, such as the headmaster of Cults Academy.

It turns out you needed a pass to get into this marquee and how your Granda got in I will never know. Joe is now standing with Aberdeen's finest oil executives, the headmaster of Cults academy and the local vicar.

So, here comes your Granda's famous trick. He's got a crowd round him, everyone laughing in stitches, the vicar included and someone in a thick American accent said, "So how do you know the headmaster of Cults academy?"
And your Granda said, "Ah, that would be telling. Wouldn't it?"
And everyone just laughed, as Joe carried on sipping champagne and eating the Michelin Star nibbles.
He could talk himself out of anything. Nobody would even call his bluff!'

He was the kind of person that you could speak to for hours without realising where the time had passed. He had the ability to talk to anyone at any level about anything. Even a vicar, as it seems. Granda was equipped with the means and ways to talk himself out of most things but trying to defuse a situation that could involve over twenty amateur football players didn't always come as easily.

'Woodside had a fantastic win at the Scottish Cup and were in very high spirits after the game. The normal protocol is that the home team invites the away team back to their local for pies and such like. So, to keep up with Scottish Cup tradition, thirty of us piled off in the coach and into our opponent's social club. We were, or at least we thought we were, directed into a large hall with tables and chairs all set out, especially for us. We go in, beers in hand, bottles of champagne and quickly get tucked into the best away team hospitality buffet we had ever seen. I mean prawn vol au vents, the lot! Anyway, fifteen minutes later and after we had taken full advantage of our host's kindness, one of the managers walks in and lets out an almighty shriek:

"OH MY GOD," she screamed at the top of her voice, "what have you done?!"
Your Granda stands up and calmly asks her, "What's wrong dear?"
"THE WEDDING," she shouts, "THE BLOODY WEDDING, YOU HAVE ALL JUST DEMOLISHED

THE EVENING RECEPTION BUFFET AND THE WEDDING PARTY WILL BE HERE IN TEN MINUTES!"

Well, if there was a hole big enough, we would have all jumped in at the same time. We were obviously gutted for the newlyweds and their guests, but we couldn't stop laughing. The manager couldn't stop screaming so we departed just before the wedding party arrived. Prawn vol au vents, yum yum!'

Granda dedicated a lot of his time to amateur football. Every Saturday, he religiously attended the Woodside games. In addition to managing his team, he took on the role of the secretary for the North of Scotland, which included planning for games that took place all over Aberdeen City and Shire every Saturday: dealing with cancelled games, getting referees in place, and logging all results

Granda being presented the Lifetime Achievement Award fin association with Amateur Football

after the games had happened. Basically, if you wanted to get through to 01224 641872 on a Saturday, you could bloody well forget about it.

But even then, Granda wasn't busy enough; his involvement in football stretched further. He was a member of several Scottish Amateur F.A. committees including the Scottish Amateur F.A. Council and the North of Scotland District Executive Committee as well as being a Life Member of the Aberdeenshire Amateur Football Association. He was awarded the lifetime achievement award for his service to these communities.

I think he saw himself as a bit of an Alec Ferguson to be honest. Except maybe with more foul language. I have fond memories of attending Woodside games on a Saturday. Well, perhaps not that fond, but I had no other choice because I was too young to stay home alone. But I value them now. It didn't matter what happened on the pitch – and a lot happened, believe me. I got to stand there and watch Granda be this great leader who people listened to and respected and in total contrast, I remember watching from the side lines as a series of bad words poured from the supporter's mouths. Every Saturday really was a spectacle. It was at those games that I learnt the Scottish appreciation of what another of our titans, Billy Connolly, calls "the poetry of swearing".

Chapter 3: Tartan Army

My Granda was fifteen when he went to his first Scotland match. He had no ticket and no transport (a situation he would become well acquainted with later in life). What he did have, was a rusty bike and the tenacity to believe that no ticket and no transport did not equate to no Scotland game. He cycled over three hundred miles from Aberdeen to Hampden and back again and with no guarantee of a ticket. If that determination doesn't set you up for life, I don't know what will. I suppose this is where the story begins.

'It was the first of many great ventures. I had to stop at Arbroath, because it was dark, and I was feeling a bit tired. I finally arrived at Hampden, only twenty minutes before the match was due to kick off.

I hadn't thought about buying a ticket in advance – I imagined that I would just be able to get one at the gate, like I did when I went to Pittodrie. So, my journey might have been in vain, considering how late I got to the stadium, but thankfully I got one from a policeman who was standing outside Hampden and he kindly agreed to keep an eye out for my bike until I came back.

The game itself didn't go very well, but that didn't really matter. I was thrilled by cheering on the Scots and I knew I was going to keep doing it.' (Joe McGunnigle, *Evening Express 1996*)

The optimism acquired from the 300-mile cycle stayed with Granda for the rest of his life; he relentlessly followed and believed in Scotland, despite some of the terrible losses they endured.

'That journey to Hampden Park in 1958 sparked a lifelong love affair with the Scottish national team.'

His unabated spirit and determination led him to become one of the world's most recognised Tartan Army foot soldiers. Granda accumulated hundreds of thousands of miles whilst following his beloved team. He attended five World Cups between 1974 and 1998 and travelled worldwide to countries such as

Granda and friends at the Kirin Cup – Japan 2006

Spain, Malta, Holland, Belgium, France, Germany, Slovenia, Sweden, Denmark, Italy, Yugoslavia, San Marino, and Japan.

It's funny that, despite the initial defeat at his first Scotland game, he went on to spend his life following them. The beauty of that one journey was that this young, naive boy with a bike had no idea what a life he was yet to lead and how much following Scotland would impact it.

There is something incredible about that journey; it represents life a little bit. If you want something, you're going to have to work hard to get it. The road might be long and a little bit rocky. You might even take the wrong track once in a while, but if you are determined, you will always get there in the end.

Granda never let anything get in the way of seeing Scotland play. He somehow made his way to Croatia in crutches and hobbled around many countries following his two hip replacements. He was even in Malta only three years ago, with a suitcase full of food supplements to pump into himself when seriously ill. But following Scotland was first nature to him and nothing would get in the way.

Boys on tour

When diagnosed with terminal cancer in October 2017, he asked the consultant if he could go to Israel a few months later to see Scotland play and, much to our surprise, it was not recommended. There weren't many obstacles that could get in the way of Granda seeing

Scotland play, but I think the most challenging one was justifying yet another trip to my Nana.

'I was round at your Granda's house and we were on his computer having a look at the prospect of going to Japan. He shouted your Nana through and said:
"Cath is it okay if me and Les go to Japan?".
She said: "Well you'll bloody go anyway, won't you? What are you asking me for?"
So, we bought flights. Technically Scotland hadn't been invited for the tournament yet but there was a good rumour that it was happening. So, we got flights for £450 return. We phoned the usual crowd and asked if they wanted to go too, and they all said they were going to wait until it was official. The very next day we were officially invited, and the same flights went up to £900!'

My Nana fully accepted that this was Granda's passion and therefor a huge part of his life. She was a very patient woman with the gentlest nature. Nana and Granda were in eternal love from a young age. Which meant Nana spent a lot of time aiding the stress of Granda when planning football trips. In fact, she probably had her fair share of stress worrying about him the whole time he was away. I remember that me and Nana would sit at their bedroom window and eagerly await Granda's return from a trip, after a week away. We would see him get out of the car, the door would close, into the building, then up the first, second and third flight of stairs. We would be waiting at the door by this point. And then, a massive hug.

We missed Granda terribly when he was gone. Even if it was only for five days. Before mobile phones came on the go, Granda would send postcards home to Nana.

Do you think there is such thing as being able to sense the love between two people in writing? I do. My Nana and Granda  were everything that love should be.

I'm not sure you could say Nana was the biggest supporter of the Tartan Army, but she was the biggest supporter of my Granda, always. Every day of her life. And he was hers.

Granda took great pride in being a Tartan Army member. It wasn't just his dedication to Scotland that people remembered him by but his character too. People were naturally drawn to Granda: he was captivating. It wasn't an uncommon sight to see people at social gatherings crowded around him, and this wasn't just in our hometown of Aberdeen, but in every country he visited with the Tartan Army too. Wherever my Granda went, people were intrigued by him.

Granda in Mexico, with some locals he befriended

Locals from foreign countries were always pleased to meet and chat with him. To them, he was the epitome of a Scotsman: bubbly, smiley, handsome, Scottish accent and dressed in a kilt. To top it off, he was probably wearing the most fascinating tartan jacket they had laid eyes upon.

Granda made space for everyone, and people could sense that. He treated everyone like a friend that he had known for a very long time. His chemistry with people was undeniable - he knew how to read every room and wear every hat. Granda left an imprint on every person he met, which even extended to winning the hearts of the entire nation of Mexico!

Mexico was one of Granda's most memorable Scotland trips. He loved everything about it there: the people, the culture, the sunshine, and the fact he managed to insinuate his way onto Mexican live TV and newspapers. He was interviewed at the Scotland game, and they loved him so much that they asked him to feature on Mexico's nightly 'World Cup Specials', and he was included in the World Cup programme every day.

Then, of course, he had to come home and tell the Aberdeen newspapers about the fact that he had been in the Mexican newspapers. By now, I'm sure you have probably guessed, Granda was not camera shy! The Aberdeen article reads, "Aberdonian Joe McGunnigle has appeared on TV more often than J.R of Dallas recently – and all because he travelled to Mexico to support Scotland".

Not only did Granda befriend the Mexican media, but local families there too. After the opening match between Bulgaria and Italy, Granda was adopted by a Mexican fan group and invited back to their house, where almost thirty people lived. It quickly became a massive party with lots of food and even more tequila.

'We met Joe when he was visiting Mexico to support Scotland in the World Cup. We saw him being filmed at the match and were very interested when we saw him. He was laughing and joking behind the camera. We knew that he was

Scottish because he was wearing a lot of the Scottish tartan. Once we got speaking with Joe and his friends, they were very kind and friendly. Joe was asking lots of questions about our home and our family. We wanted to invite him into our home and show him what our life was like. We got speaking and drinking and eating and Joe told us about his wife and what life was like in Scotland.

When I think of the night we met Joe, I think of him like our national flower, the dahlia. The dahlia is the star of the summer garden, and it is bright and colourful. I will always remember him, and we still speak about the time we spent with him and his friends. Scotland will be special to us because of this, always.'

It just so happened that the family who threw the party ran a tailoring business and even offered to make Granda a handmade banner as a keepsake. Granda chose to have a banner made for his team at the time, Waterton Thistle, and that banner travelled to many Scotland trips after that. If only he could have known then that the name of the team would soon be changing to the almighty Woodside! Saying that, he left such a lasting impression I'm sure if he had got back in touch, they would have made him another. He truly conquered the hearts of Mexico...

Waterton Thistle represents

and the Mexican media... and the media in general.

If there was ever an opportunity for my Granda to speak about his beloved Scotland in the local papers, you could guarantee he would have his best smile and tartan jacket on quicker than you could say "Scotland". Even if there wasn't an opportunity, he would create one. It really was that simple – he had the Evening Express on speed dial. Any time he was travelling, he would call up and a news team would arrive within 48 hours. My Granda became the 'go-to' guy for journalists writing about Scotland and he established a great relationship with them in the process. He had the looks, he had the banter, and he had an undeniable knowledge, which in turn provided great content for the papers.

'*How on earth can anyone come up with words good enough to pay tribute to Joe McGunnigle, Aberdeen's very own Scotland Super Fan?*

Joe and I first crossed paths many years ago – in the early 1980s – when I was secretary of Sunday Welfare League, Side Moorings Thistle and he, of course, was with his beloved Saturday Amateur team, Woodside. We competed in different leagues but played the odd friendly – if there is ever such a thing when Woodside play!

I would also have lovely chats with Joe when he appeared at Inverdee on Sunday mornings selling shin pads, boots or whatever he had managed to get a supply of at a wee table he set up outside the dressing rooms. My chats with Joe went into overdrive after I began working as a sportswriter for the Aberdeen Evening Express, in 1989.

I was already aware of his passion for the national side, so when I was asked to come up with someone local who would be willing to give a fans' perspective of the Scotland team or manager there was only ever going to be one man I was going to turn to.

Contrary to what many believe, Joe was a bit reluctant to cooperate to start with. He said he didn't want to risk being ridiculed if any article I wrote showed him in a bad light. I appreciate the fact he trusted me to treat him with fairness and respect because it meant many years of having the pleasure of writing about his travels around the globe as a member of the Tartan Army.

We covered his early days, the now famous bicycle trip from Aberdeen to Hampden he made to cheer on his beloved Scotland, and all the other adventures he enjoyed over the decades. I've lost count of how many articles we did, and how many pictures  *the Evening Express took of Joe wearing his trademark tartan suit or waving a Scotland flag. In return, I was happy to publish details of his next planned trip to cheer on Scotland and advertise any* spare seats that were available to anyone willing to go via 'McGunnigle International or Domestic Travel'.

I was fortunate to regularly run into Joe abroad, while reporting on Scotland for the Evening Express. Some of the stuff he said over the odd pint in places like Sweden, Italy, Portugal and Latvia could never be written about in a family newspaper – or a book published by his granddaughter! Joe always had me in stitches because he was a born comedian and a tremendous raconteur. I accept these are times when some comments from the past are less acceptable, but I hope you will forgive me for relating one tale.

Joe and I were enjoying a pint at a roadside bar in the Swedish town of Norrkoping, one sunny afternoon, during the 1992 European Championship finals. It was at the time of day when what appeared like hundreds of gorgeous Swedish women were making their way past us on bicycles after finishing work. Without prompting, Joe suddenly said: "Charlie, when I die, I want to be reincarnated as a Swedish bicycle seat!" A joke of its time, but at that point in 1992 it had all who heard it in tears of laughter.

On another occasion, I think it was in Italy, a police van went speeding past us, with sirens blaring and Joe said: "He will never sell any chocolate sliders at that speed!" It was an adaptation of an old Morecambe and Wise joke, but it still worked because the art is in the delivery and timing and Joe was a master of that.

There was a more serious side to Joe too.

He was always happy to provide an informed comment when asked questions during more difficult periods for the national side. I admired his knowledge and passion for Scotland, it was clear all he ever wanted was to see them winning – as long as he was there to witness it too.

My admiration for Joe rocketed when he went public with his cancer diagnosis. He showed tremendous courage as well as generosity with his decision to help raise cash for Friends of Anchor. The way he dealt with his illness was an inspiration to others and the world was indeed a sadder place when Joe passed away.

Morecambe and Wise, who I mentioned earlier, weren't above recycling things, as Joe did with their joke. Their famous signature tune 'Bring Me Sunshine' was actually an earlier hit for Willie Nelson.

The words go:

"Bring me sunshine in your smile, bring me laughter all the while.

In this world where we live there should be more happiness,

So much joy you can give to each brand-new bright tomorrow,

Make me happy through the years, never bring me any tears

Let your arms be as warm as the sun from up above,

Bring me fun, bring me sunshine, bring me love."

The song sums up Joe perfectly, he definitely brought sunshine and laughter into my world and when I think of him now it's always with a smile.'

– *Charlie Allan, Former Sports Editor, Aberdeen Evening Express.*

Chapter 4: McGunnigle International Travel

If you recognize this well-established travel brand and are still alive to tell the tale, well, I commend you. My Granda started organising domestic trips with Scotland at the age of 19. He arranged infamous coaches from Aberdeen to places like Hampden and Wembley for Scotland games. It wasn't until a bit later in life where he extended his services at an international level, where he started organising the full holiday package. A love for Scotland and his entrepreneurial instincts were exactly what set him up for a lifetime of stress, grief, narrowly avoiding being murdered and a whole lot of laughter in between.

It was 1998 and the opening ceremony of the World Cup Group stages were taking place in France. The very first game was Brazil vs Scotland, a game which no self-respecting Tartan Army foot soldier would miss, never mind the commander in chief. The only problem was that all basic flights were booked and the few that were left cost thousands of pounds. Some might have said it was impossible to get there. To Joe McGunnigle, impossible was just a word. Like a phoenix from the ashes, McGunnigle International Travel was born.

One thing that you could be assured of when booking through McGunnigh International Travel was that my Granda would try and keep costs as low as possible. Now, I'm sure you know what comes along at the price of low cost. For those that didn't travel with M.I.T, I'll let you guess. For those that did travel with M.I.T, I'll allow a few minutes for you to reminisce over some of the "accommodation" you have stayed in over the years before I take you on a trip down memory lane. Let's start with Japan 2006.

'Joe was famous for getting headline prices and this was one of his specials. He booked us into this hostel that was about an hour on the tube from Roppongi, which is where we really should have been staying. There were eight of us sharing a room. When we

opened the door, we were met by a room that was no bigger than four phone boxes. We took one look at it, and I am certain that all eight of us, including Joe simultaneously thought "What the fuck."

The 3m x 3m luxury accommodation

We complained to Joe that where our hotel was located, the tubes didn't run between midnight and 5am; as if the room size wasn't inconvenient enough. Although, the irony was that most of us didn't return home until after 5am each night anyway. Especially Joe. So, in the end, we decided that we could afford to bin the room. But not without going in and documenting the hilarious encounter first.

We told the man at the desk that we were just nipping out for a walk - with all our bags and suitcases in hand? Yeah right. He knew we weren't coming back.

I'm sorry but four bunk beds in one tiny room was not happening.

Guys wearing kilts in Japan were quite popular with the ladies and that would have killed it for those of us hoping to get lucky. I couldn't really bring a woman back to our room and say, "don't worry about the other seven, they are sleeping". Especially not with Joe rabbiting on about current political affairs at 5am. What a mood killer.

In 2022, this may be considered cultural appropriation

So, we decided that we would look for something better. We got on the train to Roppongi and stumbled across the 'Roppongi Prince'. In a matter of an hour, we had moved from a one-star hotel to a five-star hotel. We decided that we could afford to pay a few hundred pounds since the first hotel cost virtually nothing.

We all paid the same money and got allocated various rooms at the Roppongi Prince. But as it turned out, some rooms were more five stars than others. Fortunately, I was sharing with Joe, so you can guess who got the definite five-star room. Everything in our room was marble tiled. Did I mention we had a sauna?

We could have stayed in the last place, but we just thought "sod it we're having a bit of luxury". I did think to myself, "we better not tell the others about our room", because theirs were incredibly plain and had no sauna. Considering we all paid for the same thing, they were absolutely raging when they found out.'

Ok, so my Granda liked a headline price. Well in fact, he bloody loved one. He was notorious for it. The guys on my Granda's trips would spend most of their time out of their rooms anyway so it didn't matter what it looked like, they would either be at the football or exploring the city (exploring the city is a codeword for getting paralytically drunk). So, in my Granda's defence, people just didn't spend a whole lot of time at their accommodation for him to consider adding glamourous five-star hotels to the M.I.T portfolio.

Although, there is a headline price and then there was the trip to Moldova, 2004. Some lines should just never be crossed.

'Three words for Moldova. Trip from hell. So, we arrived at Aberdeen Airport and Joe was nowhere to be seen. Where was he? He had all our tickets for the game and had planned every bit of our travel, so we were quite panicked. We had to go through customs and hope he was running late and would catch up with us.

So, we got through to the other side of customs and here was Joe, sitting sipping on a pint.
I said, "Joe, why weren't you at check-in?"
He said, "Oh boys, I forgot to say, I'm travelling a different way from you."

Joe explained to us that he was flying to Turkey for a couple of hours stopover, then straight over to Moldova. Whereas us lot had a "scenic detour", which was Aberdeen to Amsterdam, Amsterdam to Bucharest, an overnight stay in Bucharest and then a "quick coach ride" from Bucharest to Moldova. That "quick coach ride" was a 233-mile journey that took sixteen hours, but Joe must have forgotten to mention that part.

At last, we were on the road to Moldova. In fact, no we weren't, because there were no roads in Moldova! Potholes everywhere. We had to stop in small gypsy villages to do the toilet in the ground. Fuck, it was horrendous. We got stopped at the border and had to wait two hours for a guard to finish his duty so we could give him a lift home, otherwise, he wouldn't let us into the country. So that was another hundred miles added on to the coach journey.

Eventually, we arrived at our hotel and here's Joe, sitting quite happy at the bar, sipping a pint, yet again!

I said, "Joe how the fuck did you manage to get the easy route here and we've been on a ramshackle for 2 days?"

He said, "I didn't think you would want to book this way; it was an extra twenty pounds!" I could have murdered him.

So, if the journey there wasn't bad enough, our coach ride home gave it a run for its money. We were driving through a tiny village and there appeared to be some sort of procession happening. As we got closer, there was a flea-bitten donkey pulling a cart that had a crucifix on it. Shit, it was a funeral. But there wasn't a coffin. There was just a body lying in this cart with some straw and a bonnet on his heed! The bus had to come to a standstill because of the procession. There were several trays of fresh food on display. This was the most edible looking food we had seen the whole trip. All in the space of a minute we had seen a dead man being carted about by a three-legged donkey and the best food we had seen in weeks. Cheers Joe!'

So that's one perspective from the Moldova trip. That perspective is through the eyes of the "scenic route" traveller. It was implied that because my Granda had the easier route to Moldova than the rest, that his trip was less shambolic. Well, put it this way, I could have written an entire book based around the stories of this one trip to Moldova but here is another perspective, which is that of my Granda and his son, Joe.

'Fucking Moldova. We had to do a detour to Istanbul to get there. When we arrived at Moldova airport, there was no luggage to be seen. My Dad just marched ahead with his kilt on, nae worried a shite if his luggage was there. I thought to myself, "Nae luggage. We're here for 10 days. How could we possibly manage?"

Day three in Moldova. Still no luggage. The place we were staying in was so poor, you wouldn't believe it. There were people walking about selling rotten apples and all electricity went off in the village at 9pm every night. At one point a truck came past our hotel and started

At least the tartan brings some colour to Moldova

tipping out rubbish and there were about four tonnes of bags of clothes amongst it.

All the locals started ripping up the bags and grabbing the clothes. We were just standing there honking... but certainly contemplating it. The locals finished rummaging through these bags of clothes and then next hurrah they were setting up stalls to sell them at. Really inconsiderate for the less fortunate (us). I ended up buying some new garments from the stalls - a shredded jacket and some trousers that were covered in rotten apples. My Dad on the other hand continued to rely on the only piece of clothing he would ever need, his kilt. I'm not sure whether he kept the same pants or went commando.

So back to the luggage. It was the end of the trip and me and my Dad were at Moldova Airport ready to go home. It wasn't like an airport you and I would know, for a start, you got stopped by gunmen on arrival. There weren't a lot of English-speaking people and, everyone had a gun, except us. Thankfully, our travel rep came with us to the airport and was going to direct us to the left luggage department. Our rep explained our situation to the guard at the entrance of the airport. The guard shook his head and put his hand out.

The travel rep said, "He wants you to pay him."

I said, "What to get into the airport?"

She said, "That's just the way it works here."

I put a few notes into his hand. His hand stayed held out.

I said, "Dad, you'd better give him some money too." but he didn't have any left.

So, I handed over some more money and the two of us were admitted into the airport. Muttering under my breath about the con artistry we had been subject to, our travel rep finally took us to the left luggage section. The man behind the lost luggage desk did not speak any English, he just shook his head a few times. We thought things looked hopeful until he put his hand out. He wanted fucking money.

"I'm not buying my clothes! It's my gear!" I said.

I looked at my Dad. "I didn't have money the first time, so I definitely don't have any now!"

So, I paid the guy, and we bought our own luggage back. The only good thing about it was that we didn't have to pay to get on the plane!

It's fair to say that Moldova was deserving of the title "the trip from hell." It turns out it had bad points for everyone and not just those that took the scenic route. Nonetheless, having no clothes would have been no skin off my Granda's back. He was notorious for packing light. *"What more do I need than a kilt?"* he would say.

Some might have argued that a limited wardrobe was a better turn of events than witnessing a donkey-led funeral, but I suppose it all comes down to personal preference. As if the nightmare fuelled trip wasn't bad enough, Scotland's qualification hopes for the World Cup 2006 in Germany were dented by a 1-1 draw to Moldova. Scotland had the best of the first half but were down a goal within twenty-eight minutes when Serghei Dadu scored a goal from six yards away. An equalizer came only three minutes later when Steven Thomspon scored a goal through the legs of the Moldovan goalkeeper. Ok hands up, favourite trip ever, anyone?

Sometimes headline prices just weren't viable, especially at bigger tournaments such as the World Cup where there were so many international travellers. So, when in doubt of paying inflated accommodation prices, why not make your own accommodation?

'France World Cup 1998. We bought a navy-blue transit van and kitted it out with the latest interior furnishings allowing it to carry seven persons in total luxury. Basically, an old sofa in the

The party wagon

back of the van and a thousand tartan hats that Joe was planning on selling. It cut costs of travelling and accommodation, so we tried to pretend it was bearable.

We travelled one thousand and fifty-eight miles to France in this bashed up old blue transit van. Saint Andrews crosses adorned every blue panel, with tartan scarves hanging out each window. Eventually we reached Gay Paree, a beautiful city that we Woodside loons had only ever seen on TV when we watched the Hunchback of Notre Dame. As for the tartan bunnets? Joe said we would easily sell them to the thousands of punters from around the globe, screaming to touch the sacred cloth that we refer to as

Tartan. All at the bargain price of £10 too. We sold about eleven in total and said, "Sod this we're off to party."

So, we ditched the van and headed down towards the Champs-Élysées. "No Scotland, no party, no Scotland, no party" were the chants we shouted as we walked down, whilst being followed by a small group of Chinese people snapping ferociously away and singing the chant too. It was hilarious. The night went by all too quickly and we ended up sitting in a wee bar drinking in a way our European neighbours had only read about in books.

It was 4am and it was pissing rain. We were sitting out on a veranda of some bar, watching the world go by and the one and only Ewan McGregor walks past soaked to the skin.

"Hey Ewan, what the hell are you doing out here in the pissing rain?"

"Alright lads," he says, "I've lost my wallet."

We thought he was winding us up.

"Get yer arse in here then and have a drink ye CU Next Tuesday," was the invite we gave him and he duly

obliged. It was at this point that Joe returned from wherever he had been; whether that was the toilet, being adopted by French nationals or selling his hats outside, you get the picture - he returned from being Joe. I called him over and said, "Joe, do you know who this is?" whilst gesturing towards Ewan. Joe turned around with a look that was all too serious to be joking and said, "Does he know who I am?"

Ewan sat with us until about 6am and borrowed enough for a taxi to get home and arranged to meet us the following day (Match Day). The next day we went to the game and out of curiosity we headed in the direction of the BBC stand in the main concourse, where Ewan had told us he would be presenting with Ally McCoist. As sure as the sun will rise in Abu Dhabi, there he was up on the stage with Coisty, true and to his every word. Next, we heard someone shouting "JOE!" No way. Ewan McGregor was shouting at us from the stage. He jumped down from the stage and took us into a small, protected area where he introduced us to his wife Eva and his Mum and Dad. "These are the lads that looked after me last night," he said.

We spent some time chatting to them, then off to the game we went, feeling like superstars."

There you have it, a trip away that started in a transit van resulted in dabbling with stardom. And although Scotland didn't get too far in the tournament (this is starting to feel like a recurring theme) with their 2-1 loss to Brazil in the first game, followed by a 1-1 draw to Norway and a 3-0 defeat to Monaco, it was a memorable trip, nonetheless.

'*During the Brazil match, Scotland went behind after just four minutes to a César Sampaio goal. Despite the setback in front of a crowd of 80,000 at the Stade de France, Craig Brown's soldiers battled bravely against Ronaldo, Rivaldo, Roberto Carlos and co, with John Collins equalizing from the penalty spot seven minutes before halftime. Both teams had chances in the second half but an unfortunate ricochet off Tommy Boyd on 73 minutes ended Scotland's hopes of beating the Champions with an own goal.*'

The only problem with having incurred these defeats at the France World Cup was how difficult it would have been to sell those hats when the morale amongst Scotland fans was so deflated. I'm sure my Granda didn't worry. After all, we had a drying room that was perfectly equipped for hat storage and I'm certain he had another business plan brewing for his tartan acquisitions.

So, back to headline prices. They are headline prices for a reason, there is no such thing as a free lunch remember. But people knew that when they booked with my Granda to expect the unexpected and that their bargain holiday may involve a 3-hour bus from their hotel to the Scotland game. Who wants a five-star hotel anyway? Character over quality.

'When we went to Italy, I can't remember the price, but it was very affordable. Joe practically had a planeload of folk. He had us in a hotel that was beyond the furthest away tube station. So, we went to the terminus of the tube station in the centre of Rome, you then got on a bus and drove for half an hour and then there was a fair walk after that. But you know, he got you there. When we arrived at the airport, the bus Joe took us on went on an excursion for hours around

Italy to get to our hotel. I don't know if it was an accident because we could see the hotel from the airport. It turned out that it was a 10-minute walk. Joe bloody loved a scenic route.'

The accommodation my Granda chose varied a lot. I think that he liked the idea of diversifying McGunnigle International Travel to keep things fun. It was a bit like a lucky dip, one trip you might be in a beautiful hotel that is hundreds of miles away from where you need to be and on the next trip you might end up somewhere very local but of very poor quality. Aren't surprises fun?

'We stayed in a quality establishment in Norway once. It was a youth hostel and apparently you had to bring your own bedding and pillows. The Tartan Army did not come equipped with bedding and pillows. So, we slept on rock hard beds without a mattress, our bags as pillows, plus the damp leaking through the walls. I think prisoners would sleep better at night than when we did.

But then I also remember a time when we stayed in a luxurious hotel in France, although it took 3 hours to get to the city centre. To be honest, Joe got us there and back in one piece and that is all that really mattered. We returned home somewhat alive.'

The variety was just a part of McGunnigle International Travel. A unique selling point if you like.

"Aye I've got us a cheap hotel in Rome, how would you boys like to go to Rome?"
"But Joe, the game's in Milan. Rome is 400 miles away?"

So, distance wasn't a deciding factor on where my Granda chose to stay. An old hang up from his days on the rusty bike, I suppose. Something else he was known to disregard was the practicality of the length of time his trips were. My Granda thought a trip to somewhere like Slovenia or Slovakia was great for fourteen days. Now, everyone else in the Scottish travel club normally chose to go away for 3 or 4 days, because that is all their work or wives would allow. But my Granda thought that a couple of weeks in Slovenia was cool. Well, it probably would have been cool if you didn't have a job or if your main holiday every year was following Scotland and not your family holiday.

'Right so a few days away with Scotland was fine for everyone else but Joe normally ran ten-day trips, you know. You would maybe have five days first and the Scotland game on the sixth day. We were always in the country about five days before everyone else. Another supporter group would arrive from Aberdeen the day before the match and we would show them all over the place because we had been there for a week already, speaking the language and everything!

So, after the actual game, everyone would be flying home the next day but we would still have four days left in the country, which was a serious blow if we lost. We could have done it in two days, but Joe did it in eight. Why? Because he was Joe McGunnigle. Why the hell not? "Aye but we got a good deal on the hotel" he would say!'

In the forty years that my Granda organised Scotland games, he established a network in many countries. He kept in touch with people that he met too (with a bit of technical assistance from myself). Some of you might remember the trusted desktop computer that was in his bedroom at Nelson Street; many people sat by his bedside in his bedroom "office". He tried his best to stay in touch and thankfully people remembered him, so when he was ever going back to somewhere he had already been before, he would get in touch with accommodation and services that he had used, to try and negotiate a reasonable price, naturally. Well, that is providing they wanted him and his entourage of foot soldiers back in their premises.

'We went over for a Scotland game to Prague with McGunnigle International Travel. We were staying in Prague (believe it or not) but we travelled there via bus which went through Germany, so we planned to stay a night in Germany on the way to Prague and then another night in Germany on the way home again.

On the way home, we were in the coach that was taking us back to our hotel in Germany. We were about ten minutes away and the hotel phoned Joe and said we weren't getting back because one of the boys had pissed on the mattress. Anyway, Joe, the diplomat is on the phone to the hotel. "Nae bother. I'll get it sorted boys."

He rounded up money from everyone on the bus and paid for about 10x the cost of a mattress. He put his suit on and walked into the hotel to present the money to replace the mattress and negotiate our entry. Low behold we were admitted back in once again! McGunnigle magic.'

Granda very rarely had any problems with any of the guys. The Tartan Army as a whole have an upstanding reputation in other countries. They are clean and respectful and do not cause too much trouble, after a national push for better behaviour at matches in the 1980s.

The term 'Tartan Army' was coined in the 1970s, to describe the crowds who would stand on the terracing at Hampden to see Scotland or at Wembley when they played England. The fans were criticised at that time for their hooligan behaviour after invading the pitch at Wembley and destroying the goal posts after Scotland beat England 2-1 in 1977.

My Granda was part of the positive steer in direction away from that type of behaviour, and always tried to ensure that the guys on his trip were abiding by his expectations and were respectful to their hosts. But although there was a limited amount of people problems, he still had his fair share of problems... that he got people involved in.

'We went to The Faroe Islands on a plane Chartered by your Granda. When we were due to come home it became apparent that the Scottish teams' plane had damaged its landing gear when landing in the Faroes. Your Granda stepped in and very kindly offered them our plane first. The team accepted and we all then had to sit in the Faroes Airport for an additional 8 hours until the plane dropped the Scottish National team in Glasgow and then came back for us. By the time we got back to Aberdeen, we had been awake for more than 2 days and were seriously unwashed. Still, it was a great couple of days and one of my favourite memories as a fan. I don't know what your Granda got as a thank you from the team, but we all got some pictures with players, and I still show people my picture with Craig Gordon from that day!'

Well, the proof is truly in the pudding. There is no length my Granda would not have gone to support Scotland. There is no distance he would not have travelled, no mountain he would not climb and no transport he would not willingly dispense on behalf of forty men who were desperate to get home. Thankfully the transport he did dispense was in fully functioning operation, unlike another occasion.

'We were in Portugal and Joe hired a minibus to get us from our hotel to the airport. The minibus broke down, so we all had to get out and push it! We managed to bump start it. So, it started, then it cut out, then it started, then it cut out. Then the bonnet was open, we were putting water in gods knows where. Of course, Joe comes in about to try and do his bit. "You all go back on the bus; I'll get it sorted." He turned the key, it fucking started. We never heard the end of that one. Course he was the one that fixed it. How did you do that Joe?

"That would be telling."

That wasn't the first time either. When we were in Malta, a bus that Joe had hired for us broke down going up a hill and you best believe who was delegated the task of pushing the bus up the hill and who was delegated the task of delegating the tasks!'

But what Scotland fan would remember that 2016 trip to Malta and their key memory as pushing a bus up a hill? It may have been worth it anyway, because Scotland had a triumphant start to their World Cup Qualifying campaign with a 5-1 victory! It may be remembered from when Snodgrass gave Scotland the lead with a deep cross-shot, until Albert Effiong achieved a goal with a header, bringing the hosts back level. Martin brought Scotland back ahead in the second half and just as things were in close range, Snodgrass scored the third goal from the spot after he was awarded a questionable penalty. Fletcher came in from substitution and smashed the fourth goal for Gordon Strachan's side, before Snodgrass scored the fifth and final goal of the game, making it a memorable hat-trick for Scotland fans. A bit of good karma for pushing that bus up the hill.

What I remember about the trips is that it didn't matter if you were abroad, going to Hampden or Wembley. My Granda would fill his bus or plane up, whether it was forty or one hundred people he took with him, with the promise of quality digs, luxury travel and a ticket for the game.

So, we've covered the travel, which was typically ramshackle buses that broke down, and the digs: some like Rising Damp and others like Fawlty Towers. Then that just leaves the tickets for the games, which most of the time, he never had. But you didn't get to know that until 5 minutes before the game.

You couldn't get angry at this guy

"'Dinna worry about your tickets; I'll give you your tickets when we get there." Joe would tell us at Aberdeen Airport. We would get to our hotel and still no sign of our tickets. The day before the game would arrive, "Joe, can we get our tickets?" "No, no" he would say. "I'll keep them because you'll just lose them." Sometimes he would put it off and you would realise there was something up. Especially when you would

see him approaching people in the street walking up to the game.

"Is that spare tickets he's selling?" Joe would ask.

"Why are you asking like, Joe?" we would say. "Spare tickets, it's just good to have them." Or some hilarious shite like that. "Okay, Joe, how many tickets have you got?"

The man with the plan

"How many of us are there here?"

"40," I said, "how many tickets have you got?"

"14," he said.

"14…. Are you joking me? 40 people and you've got 14 tickets." And 10 of them he had just bought a few minutes before.

"Aye but I'm meeting a boy called Alan from the Scottish Travel Club and he's got tickets," Joe said.

"That's good Joe, how many does he have?"

"I think he has four." 22 tickets short still.

It quite often worked out though because the closer

you got to the game you started losing men. People were so drunk that they didn't go to the game, or they got lost. I don't know how Joe got away with it sometimes. I genuinely don't know how he didn't get murdered fae somebody.'

Despite the occasional blunder, my Granda had a loyal band of followers on every trip he planned. One time on a trip down to Hampden, he had a bus full of people and halfway there he announced, *"Tickets... No, I've not got any tickets. But I do have everything under control."*

People didn't book with him for perfection, they booked with him for the experience; for the fun and the camaraderie that was guaranteed in every trip. There may have been mishaps that prior planning could have helped but Joe McGunnigle didn't need a plan. He had a way of making things work themself out. He was a smooth talker, fast thinker, and great drinker. And what problems can't be solved with those characteristics considered?

The McGunnigle International Travel fan base

fluctuated over the years, with people coming and going and of course some sad circumstances such as the loss of a foot soldier. It wasn't an easy task, to go on a Scotland trip without one of the comrade's that had been there for every win, for every loss. I can't begin to imagine the empty presence at games.

One of my Granda's greatest friends, who you could always rely on to be by his side, especially on Scotland trips, was the late Stevie Forbes. A gentle giant and well-adored member of the Tartan Army. I know first-hand my Granda lost

Granda and his boys heading off from Aberdeen Airport

many close companions from his Tartan community, but he always ensured that nobody would forget them and that their stories would live on. Some of the guys that followed my Granda simply had to retire. Because even when Granda reached his sixties, he showed no signs of slowing down. In fact, I think he accelerated!

'In the early days when I started following Scotland, it was Joe's trips I would always go on. Joe's trips are the ones you wanted to be on. And I did a lot of them; in fact, I'm still convinced I'm recovering from most of them. As I got older and wiser, I realised it would be best for my own wellbeing to just meet up with Joe's group there. By the time I was thirty-six I couldn't hack his antics any longer!'

Crazy times? Yes. But they are most certainly cherished times too.

'Joe's trips were legendary. Joe's trips are the ones we speak about until 5am and it's time to go to bed but we can't stop laughing. They would have been nothing without him. My life would have been nothing without him. I spent 70% of my time planning to go on Scotland trips or actually being on them and so that meant a lot of time with Joe. Going away is just not the same without him but I'm so glad that I enjoyed those years of travelling with him and learning all that he had to give.'

When my Granda wasn't occupied planning

international excursions, it was likely he was planning a domestic trip, sometimes to Wembley but more often than not, to Hampden. My Granda's "luxury executive" coaches were often the platform where he became known by new people. He had been planning coach trips to Scotland games since he was nineteen years old.

In the later years when Scotland were popular, he would often have two or three full buses heading to Hampden from the William Wallace statue. He filled his buses either with people he knew or with local people looking to make their way down to a match. His prices were very reasonable too. He may have tried to sell you some merchandise with inflated costs on the way there to cover his own but nonetheless

The usual suspect's meeting point

they were reasonable prices. And let's be fair, it wasn't just a seat on the bus you were paying for. You were paying to be part of Joe's bus, to experience first-hand a true Scotsman and the enthusiasm he had for his team. My Granda was a first for a lot of people. Many guys went on their first Scotland trip with him, some as adults and some as young as children.

'Your Granda's bus took me to my first ever Scotland game. He was an inspiration to all of the young folk who would go down on his buses and listen to the stories that he would share. Joe helped a lot of us understand what supporting Scotland was really about. Win or lose, his spirits remained high and hopeful. We admired that so much.'

That to me is incredibly special. The people whose first Scotland game was with my Granda really didn't know how impactful it would be. They could have ended up on any bus, but they ended up on his. I have no doubt that whatever age they are now, they will remember that first trip fondly. And if they're lucky enough, they might just remember the wise words that he told them.

My Granda relished every part of organising these trips, he was the only man I've ever known to have a seating plan on a supporters' bus. Not that the seating plan was always adhered to, but he loved to have one anyway. On the contrary, very few rules on "Joe's bus" were adhered to.

'Joe always said no alcohol allowed on the buses but of course we would smuggle some on anyway. If he caught you with it, he would let you keep it under one condition. Whatever it was, you had to share it with him!'

So, in summary, you should always obey the rules. Unless the rules can be bent in your favour and in return you get free booze. Ethical? No. Practical? Yes. But rules are made to be broken and Joe McGunnigle had so much credibility that anyone would respect whatever rules he made... or broke.

'I travelled on Joe's buses from a young age. It was always considered a privilege to pay £20 for a six-hour standing trip just to be on his bus. I later joined the police and being on Joe's bus was– let's just say a conflict of interest!

I started running my own buses but even then, running them was always risky with boys sneaking drink on (we all snuck booze on in plastic bottles, but you still got the numpties that brought glass and tins). Joe started putting my bus in his name just in case I got into trouble, and it reflected on me and my career. I'll always remember that. I eventually stopped running my own bus and went back onto Joe's, this time getting a seat every time. I remember a few years back running into Joe in the Pittodrie bar and ended up sitting with him till closing. He had been keeping track of my police career and commented on how well I had done since being the lad that used to stand on all his buses.'

People will remember Granda for a multitude of reasons. Some will remember him for the stories he told, some will remember him for his larger-than-life personality, and some will remember him for how he impacted their lives, but few will remember him as the man who invented toilets on a bus:

'I swear to you, Joe invented toilets on buses. We used to complain going down the road to Hampden that

there was so many toilet stops. What did you expect with a bus load of heavy drinkers? Everyone used to complain because sometimes we were stopping at every second turnoff. One time we were heading off to Hampden on Joe's bus; we met at the William Wallace statue as usual.

Joe was standing proudly with a Marks and Spencer's carrier bag. I said to him, "Joe what's in the bag?"
He said, "I've sorted the pish problem."
He then pulled a funnel out of the carrier bag and indicated the funnel towards the opening of the carrier bag. The bus didn't stop once on the way to Hampden.

I'm starting to see exactly why he called it "luxury, executive travel". Anything can be luxury if you put the word "luxury" before it!

McGunnigle International Travel – Est. 1998

McGunnigle Domestic Travel – Est. 1961

Photos

Where is your signature grin Joe?

Nana and Granda - Frankfurt Airport June 1974

From left to right: Margaret (sister-in-law), Paddy (brother in law), Tommy (brother), Cathy (sister), Cath (wife), Granda

Granda and Nobby Gordon

There's the signature grin!

Granda "on duty" following Scotland

Argentina World Cup - 1978

World Cup Qualifier – Cyprus, 8th February 1989

The '80's called...

Belgium 2001 – World Cup Qualifiers

Granda cheering on his sister Cathy dancing

The Tartan Army in Gay Paree

World Cup - Italia 90

European Championships - Sweden 15th June 1992

Granda and his brother Frank at an Aberdeen match

Me, Granda, Karen and Misty

After Woodside won the Premier League!

Granda and Misty at the Ballater Highland Games

Photos

Granda with his friend Les - A troublesome duo

Granda's home cooked meal for guests

Granda with his Woodside boys after winning the Premier League for a third year running

Granda with his daughter Karen

Family trip to St. Andrews

Granda with some BRAVE brothers

95

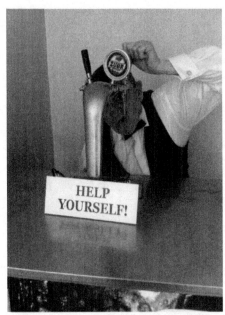

Granda at his Grandson Neil's wedding in Poland, taking "Help yourself" to another level

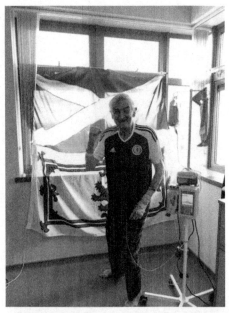

Granda not allowing being in hospital to stop him from watching Scotland in style

Granda and me celebrating Misty's 9th Birthday

Granda on stage at BRAVE 2018

Photos

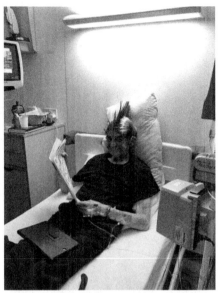

"Instead of losing my hair, chemotherapy has done the opposite", Granda joked

Granda heading off to be a model

Premier Division champions are Woodside!

Watching Scotland at home in true comfort

Granda at Rachael's wedding. He had been put to bed but climbed out of his window to come back to the party

Granda and Misty enjoying the Ballater scenery

Granda with Dod (left) and James (right) watching a Scotland game at Nelson Street

Granda with his cousins at his 75th Birthday party

Left to right: Me, Granda, Uncle Graeme, cousin Rachael and John, Auntie Karen and cousin Chris – Rachael & John's wedding

Me and Granda at my 21st Birthday party

Tartan superfan Joe on road to Wembley again

IN more than 30 years, Joe McGunnigle has never missed a Scotland-England game. Joe, from Aberdeen, had dashed home from work to catch the European Championship draw on TV.

"I was too late but when I arrived my wife was shouting out of the window," he said.

"To be honest, I was hoping for nice wee trip to Dublin to play Eire, or something a bit more exotic...

Even if Scotland had drawn far-flung Israel, Joe, 56, would have been there — he has travelled the world as part of the Tartan Army.

Still, he's more than happy to take on the Auld Enemy.

"It's the oldest football

gave me one outside the ground and said he'd look after my bike."

The game that "sticks out a mile" is the 3-2 victory at Wembley in 1967, a year after England won the World Cup.

"That was a cracker," said Joe, a kitchen designer. "We put their place that d Even when Scot banned for scalp Wembley in 197 made it to the g south.

"You got there the place war He has alrea bus for the Hampden to fill one I'm conf over two our figh

● EVE McGun there f tick an

Scotland superfan Joe won't be in pink

● BRAVEHEART: Joe McGunnigle was shocked by the price of the new pink strip.

SCOTLAND superfan Joe McGunnigle was today stunned by the news it will cost an astonishing £84.97 to buy the national side's new salmon-pink away kit.

Aberdeen-based Joe was already unhappy at the prospect of the Tartan Army becoming the "Pretty in Pink Brigade" by wearing the bright new tops.

He believes the SFA have committed a second own goal by announcing fans will have to fork out almost £85 for a complete set of shirt, shorts and socks.

"With prices like that I think I will just stick by the

● PRETTY IN PINK: Scotland's new away strip will cost £84.97

jersey I bought to go to the 1974 World Cup finals in Germany," said Joe. "The prospect of the Tartan Army being

described as 'looking pretty in pink' was already giving me a headache.

"We would have been open to all sorts of jokes.

"The price might ease those fears a little because I just can't see many fans paying that sort of money for the kits.

"Posers who don't go to games might like it though — it seems the perfect sort of thing to wear when they go on holiday to Spain in the summer."

Manufacturers Umbro remain confident the Tartan Army will snap up the strips at any price.

"We're sure it will be a big hit," said spokesman Simon Marsh.

Sporting Bravehearts... Superfan for Bannockburn

Mel starring in epic happy hour

NORTH east Scotland fans will next week raise a toast to the actor whose heart is one of our brave hearts over the border.

Aberdeen's Sports man's Club, Queen Road have decided to put in their road to show the real England Euro '96 Club fever as members of the more brave hearts and their pals come out for a day to the Spa Inn, Bucksburn.

And as draw will available across the rejoice at Happy Hour the barmaid cum Wil and's own ancestor Mel Gibson's Wallace screen actor to stir up the fans of the Scottish bus side

come to see the game on the big screen, said a club spokesman.

Bravehear is about to cause it's about Scots beating the forces of England over superior En force.

While the English paid dirty tricks to get Wallace in the end.

"But we are candidates for being de ou such rotten de Kevin Keegan

We are now watching Bravehear is the very sort of hero in the right screening wearing a kilt draw in remin us drawn to help aid the ring of the battle.

As an added bonus anyone now attending the club who is wearing a kilt will be given a free drink.

Joe leading Tartan Army marathon

SCOTLAND superfan Joe McGunnigle is being by the trip to the of a Scotland marathon ever Scotland v English football the bus now

The 16-year-old is also part of a massive tour that is following the in their Euro 96 campaign.

The Tartan Whizz plans a three-city tour taking in the Wembley clash on Saturday, the Holland clash immediately afterwards and the

the end will enjoy clashes of a superb to it the one they've been looking forward to as a planned a longer trip through to the

Specialist Sounds

Guaranteed Quality at the lowest Low prices
33 South Colege Street,
The Arcade Room.
Mobile: 0797 6400
Mobile: 01224 211

LADIES NIGHT!

Scottish Premier U21
Youth League
Monday 8th November 7pm
ABERDEEN U21
v DUNDEE UTD U21

it out

ought I might struggle to e bus but the Germany f looks likely to rule that ' he said.

very Scotland fan I have ken to is buzzing after the win.

It has really left us conient that we can someing from the game in Prague well."

Anyone wanting to book a eat on the bus now will have to move quickly. Joe can be contacted on Aberdeen 643872.

● JOE MCGUNNIGLE: amazed at the amount of fans wanting to go the Czech Republic for Scotland's victory over Germany in midweek.

Chapter 5: I get by with a little help from my friends

A true friend is hard to come by, but my Granda was one. He was loyal, he was caring, and he was definitely the kind of person you would want as a friend, at least until you desperately needed sleep at 5am and he was insistent on "one more" whisky. He had an endless supply of generosity and would have given his last pound to someone who needed it more, even if it was

Granda and the late Billy Forsyth

someone he didn't know. In fact, he would have gone beyond that.

He had this ability to shed light on any bad situation and help others see that things aren't always as bad as they first thought. His kindness and his gallus humour, matched with an infectious laugh, formed the man that made a lasting impact on every single person he met.

'*My friend Patrick and I met Joe in 2005. He was running a bus from Lithuania to the Scotland game in Belarus. Since this, we have met up with Joe all over Europe at many other Scotland games. It was always good to see him.*

The bus Granda ran from Lithuania

It was a pleasure to know him, and we always had a good laugh together. We really enjoyed his great character. You had a special Granda.

We bumped into each other outside a pub in Luxemburg in 2012, when Scotland had a friendly game there. When he spotted Patrick and I, he came running over and after a big hello, he said, "I knew I would meet my two German friends here, so I brought something for you."

We were very surprised and wondered what was coming next...

He took off his famous tartan jacket and then took off a Scotland jumper that was underneath. This revealed that he was wearing another Scotland jumper, which he took off and handed to Patrick, which revealed yet ANOTHER Scotland jumper which he took off and handed to me. After that, he put back on the first Scotland jumper and his tartan jacket and we enjoyed some beers

Granda with Mario, Patrick and his friend Gerrit

together. He was wearing a total of three Scotland jumper's and a jacket, just so that on the off chance he saw us, he could give us them. He must have been absolutely sweating. But that is just the kind of person he was. A great guy, who we will never forget.'

Whether he had known a person all of his life or he had just met them, my Granda made time for everyone. It wasn't necessarily the amount of time he gave each person but instead what he did with that time. My Granda was a strong believer in time being the most precious thing you could give to a person. When you give your time to someone, you are giving them a fraction of your life that you can never take back. He gave so much of his life to other people in different ways and although he maybe didn't realise the lasting impact of it when he was here, it is so clear to me that he was and continues to be an influence on many people.

'This is a wee story about your Granda and the kindness he would show to strangers. One of the strangers was me when I was only eighteen years old. My parents had a new kitchen installed by Joe when he worked as a kitchen designer. Once he had completed it, he popped back round a few days later to make sure everything was okay, and my parents were happy with the fitting and quality.

I just happened to be coming round the corner on my way from my work as Joe was leaving. I had never *met him before and my Mum introduced us to one another. We were chatting and naturally the topic turned to football. I was a big lover of football, which made it an enjoyable natter. Joe asked me if I played football and I explained to him that I had played all throughout my younger days at school at Champion Street and then with the Juveniles at Aberdeen Lads Club but I never moved to junior because I struggled to find a team and so lost touch with playing the game. Joe then said, "Right loon come and play with my team, I'll see you right."*

I was quite apprehensive as I had no idea what team he even ran, and I had literally just met the guy. But within minutes of meeting him, something felt right. He could see that I was nervous but could sense that I was keen.

He said, "Okay son, I'll pick you up on Saturday at 12.30pm".

I gave him a wee smile and said,

"I might be shite for all you ken."

He chuckled and said,

"Well, we'll soon find oot!"

I then thanked him and explained how grateful I was for the opportunity, but I wouldn't be able to because I didn't have any football boots.

"What size are yi loon?" he asked. I told him. Joe then popped open his boot and handed me a pair of football boots of the correct size.

"There you go, sorted! Now I've given you a team, I've given you boots, you've nae excuse now so I'll see you on Saturday. Don't let me down!"

How could I let down such generosity and a gesture that was so kind? I was blown away. Joe never knew me but could tell I wanted to play and just lacked a little confidence after not playing for a bit. I then realised it might be worth knowing what team I was going to be playing for. Joe told me the team was Woodside and that they were a great bunch of guys, and I would be totally fine.

Joe was right. I only played one season with Woodside, but I had a great time and had the chance to meet some brilliant guys. What a laugh I had during my time there, the banter was brilliant. Joe was a top man and an even better manager. He always knew how to get the best out of you. Since playing for Woodside, I never stopped playing football until my 30's. I thanked Joe every time I crossed his path. He was an absolute legend, and I will be forever grateful for the opportunity he gave to someone he didn't even know.'

My Granda was a very giving person, even if he didn't always have a lot to give, whether it was a gift, a favour, or time. He always encouraged me to be the same. It was a ritual that when visiting someone's house for dinner, I must always bring a small gesture as a thank you. When I was twelve years old, my Granda would drop me off at a friend's doorstep. I would sheepishly knock at the door and hand over a bunch of flowers or a box of chocolates and say, "These are for your mum." Something which I found incredibly awkward. This, I am now thankful for.

Granda didn't do anything to make himself look good either; everything he did, he did with sincerity and compassion. When he visited impoverished countries, he would always bring an extra suitcase full of my old toys to hand out to the children there. He was incredibly humble, for he understood struggle.

'The thing about Joe is, he could dance with anybody. Whether it was a room full of intellects or a room full of homeless men. He brought everyone to his level. He gave anyone a winning chance. He championed the underdog. From the bottom of my heart, he was one of life's greatest.'

That's probably the one thing I loved the most about my Granda. Writing this book has illustrated just how many others loved that about him too. He passed no judgement. Everyone, despite their life's circumstances, deserved an equal opportunity to be understood. He looked at everyone the same way he looked at himself.

Another thing that I admired so much about my Granda was his ability to move with the evolving ideologies of society. I do not mean to tarnish all people of his era but there were definitely people of his age that refused to accept these shifts. My Granda was very accepting of change.

But he also had a lot of traditional values that mostly involved being respectful of other people, helping others, and being faithful to those you love. Not to forget, you never phone anyone after 10pm at night, and when food is presented, wait until everyone is seated before eating. And you especially never leave the dinner table until everyone has finished! But I like to think that when I have children, I will implement and pass those on too. All in all, my Granda had a fairly modern approach to life. If you were a nice person, that was what would matter the most.

'Your Granda was one in seven billion. He was an incredible man with whom I shared not only a love for our country, but its freedom too. Scotland, the only nation he thought was worth being part of. I'm not from Aberdeen and he was so happy when I met an Aberdonian.

Your Granda was there when I got engaged at the Croatia game in June 2013, which we won! He thought that was the reason that Scotland did so well and told me to get engaged at every game. I was so glad he shared that special moment with us. There is no one else's magic I'd rather have had there in that moment.

When I got pregnant, he demanded that I start bringing the baby to Scotland games as soon as possible. Your Granda was delighted when we got pregnant. He was genuine in his pride, and we promised him we would make our baby part of the Tartan Army. Joe was so proud of being

Granda with Alissa

a Scot, it was contagious. It was heart-warming to know someone felt like me. He had so much passion for his country and people. He was the first person I thought of when we qualified for the Euro's.

He is the first person I think of during every game. He was a legend and I'm truly grateful to have met him, and I wish my wee boy had met him too. If Mackay grows up to be half the man Joe was, I will be the happiest mum in the world. I'll be taking Mackay to games and marches and I'm sure your Granda will be smiling down.'

My Granda was a friend to so many people. I often wondered how he remembered so many names, especially in his later years. Well, the truth is (sorry Granda), he didn't. If he couldn't remember someone's name, he would say:

"Oh, you'll need to remind me of your name again.."
And someone might have said, *"It's Mike."*
And he would say, *"Oh Mike don't be silly, I knew that! I meant your last name?"*

It was no wonder that he forgot the occasional name, with so many likely to be floating about in his head; his network was just enormous. He was a known character from many places and times of his life, such as being brought up in Woodside, his work in various fields across the city, his political involvement and of course his dedication to amateur and Scottish football from a young age.

Growing up, it was an ache going anywhere with Granda because he would always bump into one or ten people that he knew, even on holiday in Tenerife. And it was never a quick hello either, more of a half-hour reminiscence. It is a testament to my Granda of course because I can't imagine that anyone would stand and chat with me for longer than five minutes. Although, the people I am referring to are those that my Granda didn't see very often and were genuinely delighted to have a proper catch up. His friends that saw him on the regular and were often victim to the antics of Joe McGunnigle might not have viewed him in the same light!

'We were at Frankfurt Airport and Joe was complaining of sore feet. We had a while to wait for our flight, so we found a couple of seats and I went off to get us a bottle of wine. We were drinking from these fancy plastic glasses and a few wines later we realised we had been sitting right in front of a pedicure booth. Your Granda was a bit boozy by this point but when he saw it, he was over there before he even stood up. He sat down and plopped his crabbit feet in the basin and a young woman started massaging, buffing and cutting his taes, the whole works. His kilt was rolled up past his knees. We were about one inch away from knowing if he had gone full Scotsman or not. Next thing, he shouted at me to come over and in the poshest accent you could imagine he said:

"Dod, can you bring me over a glass of wine? If it's not too much of an inconvenience."

I obliged and delivered the wine. So, here's Joe now sitting like he was at the bloody Ritz - a beautiful young woman at his feet (actually she was very large and German but regardless), sitting there sipping his wine like he was the Queen of Sheba. And as you could guess, I had to go back every time to top him up. Pure luxury.'

His friends loved his company, and he loved and appreciated theirs in equal measure. Granda had this extraordinary way of engaging with others. Having that kind of personality is not something you could acquire. He was gifted with this incredible ability to talk, listen, and make people laugh until their insides were sore. He really cared, and it made his day whenever he could find that bond with people through communication.

'It wasn't until we got involved in football that I got to know Joe properly. Then the phone calls at half past two in the morning started rolling in when Cathy had gone away to her bed because she was fed up with him spikin aboot politics. We used to put the world right

though. He was such a character. So well liked throughout Aberdeen.'

Talking of putting the world right, my Granda was often known to be someone that the younger Tartan Army supporters looked up to or sought advice from. I like to think that his moral compass was very well aligned. But you could imagine that such a moral compass provoked conflict when witnessing some of the naughty antics of the younger guys. And giving my Granda's likeliness to share his views, this was no exception.

'The one memory that sticks in my mind was the night after the Scotland match in Japan 2006. We had been out celebrating because Scotland had won the Kirin Cup. After we got back to our hotel room, Joe was giving me this lecture about depravity and debauchery. Just about everyone I knew on a Tartan Army trip was chasing after a bit of skirt, but Joe was dead against it. So, he could definitely stand from a moral high ground on people "hooring about" I think was his exact phrase.

Which might not have been so bad if I hadn't have taken a lady back already. What a way to kill the mood. Thankfully she didn't speak any English so didn't translate Joe's disapproval. But that was my strike from Joe. Once she left, he was giving me that speech until about three o'clock in the morning and I remember thinking,

Granda and Cammy

"When is it going to stop?" But he actually went back out and went down to the bar, probably to find his next target!'

I always remember my Granda talking about his fond memories of Japan. One of them being the celebrations after Scotland's win of such an international trophy. It's no wonder they celebrated so hard due to the well-deserved success. Well.. They won at 0-0 but due to their previous 5-1 win in the tournament against Bulgaria, they were trumped the winners of the Kirin Cup 2006; in true Scotland style. I remember the festivities just for qualifying for the tournament!

Every success was sung by my Granda. Even the downfall and defeats were celebrated too. That to me is a true Scotland fan: a man that honours his team's efforts every single time without doubt and who would relentlessly turn up to their next game with an effervescent enthusiasm despite any previous losses.

My Granda travelled to almost every Scotland game and following them gave him the opportunity to see countries that he would never normally visit, such as Japan, Slovenia, Mexico and Ukraine. So, when the opportunity arose to travel to America, bearing in mind he had never been before, it seemed too unlikely that the Tartan Army General wasn't going to be in attendance.

'Scotland were heading to Jacksonville, America for a friendly in May 2012. When I booked to go, Joe told me, "I'm not going, I'm definitely not, it's far too expensive."
I always thought it was odd for Joe to be missing a game. When there was a will, there was always a way with him, but he kept insisting he wasn't going. Strangely, he was really interested in where I was

staying and what flights I was going on, but I didn't click on.

A few weeks before the trip I asked him again if he was sure he didn't want to come.

"I'm just not going, and I don't want to speak about it."
He carried out than charade for almost a year.

When I arrived in Florida and dumped my stuff at the hotel. Who was the first person I saw? Of course... It was Joe. And I tell you, he looked like an overgrown cub scout, geared up in a dress shirt, beige shorts with the Joe classic: socks and sandals and a beaming smile on his face. He had planned all this time to be there and surprise me. That was Joe, he loved winding up his friends and I'll tell you something, he was really good at it!'

And it wasn't just his friends that my Granda liked winding up but basically any member of the public. If you merely existed, you were eligible for a Joe McGunnigle wind-up. One of the funniest memories I have of him being on the wind-up is when he went into Royal Bank of Scotland and asked for one-hundred pounds worth of one-pound notes.

He then proceeded to go to various places for lunch and attempt to pay with said one-pound notes. The high for him was seeing the confused look on the waiter's face. They would normally stutter and say something along the lines of, *"I'm sorry we can't accept this."*

Then next hurrah, Granda would produce his Samsung Galaxy that was temperamental at the best of times and prove via Google Search that his one-pound notes were in fact a legal tender. And so, he paid twenty-five pounds in one-pound notes.

Another of his favourites was walking our little Jack Russell Terrier Misty into shops such as Debenhams or Primark and waiting to be told he couldn't bring his dog inside. He would then pretend to be blind and explain to the sales assistant that Misty was his guide dog and would stumble around on his way out.

'I travelled to my first away game with him to the Czech Republic on a bus from the Pittodrie Bar in '99. My favourite story was when we were in a foreign airport and lots of people were taking photos of us in our kilts. We got chatting to this old American couple

and Joe asked where they were from. They both replied, "L.A." in a strong West Coast accent.

Joe said, "I used to stay in L.A."

"Really, Los Angeles?!" they said.

Joe looked at them straight in the face and replied, "No, Logie Avenue!"

Although my Granda loved to joke, there were definitely some situations he got the lads into where they did not quite see the funny side.

'We were down to see Scotland play at Wembley and we were speaking away to some bin men. It just so happened that Joe was two tickets short (shock). One binman said, "I'll give you two tickets for the game if you help us with the bins tomorrow."

"WE'LL DO IT!" said Joe, with no hesitation.

So, the day after the game, 4 of Joe's boys were walking about Camden Town, emptying dustbins with a treacherous hangover. It was fucking terrible.

In fact, another time when we were meant to be going to Wembley, we were in the pub speaking to the cockney boys and one of them said to Joe, I'll take you to Wembley for £1 each. Joe agreed and all eight of us hopped in the back of this van. We had been sitting in the van for half an hour when Joe said, "We must be near now," as he banged through to the driver. It was strange because we couldn't hear any noise from the football grounds. The van didn't appear to be moving so Joe fiddled about with the lock and bust the back door open. We were exactly in the same space where we got into the van. We had been locked in it and hadn't even moved at all, but we didn't even realise. Thankfully we still made it to the game but that was one of those times I could have killed Joe; he was in hysterics. But then the next thing, we were all in hysterics. Joe had an infectious laugh and sense of humour. There was no escaping it.'

My Granda might have induced some situations which weren't quite as funny then as they are now, but they have definitely aged well. The funny thing about mistakes is that life doesn't come with instructions and neither does running a domestic/international travel company, so we must forgive. There were good times, bad times, and a lot of laughing but all in all, my Granda was a good friend, and everybody knew it.

'One night, we were all in the Golden Gate square in Kiev and suddenly a large group of skinheads came out of nowhere without any warning and set about the Tartan Army. They had baseball bats and were throwing rocks and bottles with the intention of hurting us. I wasn't with your Granda at that point. Thankfully we all ran away, but my good friend Dave was just back from a broken ankle and couldn't run so well. He got caught up in the mess and had a couple of skirmishes with the skinheads. The end result was that his Scotland top got ripped off, which left him topless in what was baltic weather and his glasses also got smashed. Dave can't see at all without his glasses.

Your Granda found Dave struggling after the skinheads had left. He managed to get Dave a new Scotland top and Scotland jumper and amazingly a new pair of glasses so that Dave could continue with his night. He stayed with him until we all found each other again. That's maybe nae as funny as the other stories but it is definitely one that we both remember Joe for, he was a very, very kind man who looked out for us all.'

My Granda's "no man left behind attitude" wasn't limited to football games. He always put other people before himself, off the pitch too. Even if helping others didn't always work out, he could never have said that he didn't try. Caring about other people ran right through the man's veins.

'I have been to rock bottom. And I have come back and went down again. And I'm not afraid to say that. And the only reason I'm not afraid to admit is because Joe was the only one that didn't treat me how everyone else did. Joe was there no matter how many times I fucked up. When I had no money, when I had nowhere to go, he held a hand for me to grab onto. Even when I didn't deserve one. As a young guy with no Dad, Joe was the next best thing, in fact – better. Joe got me involved in amateur football when I was young because I was in a lot of trouble and hanging out with the wrong crowds.

He saved me, and I didn't even ask him to. He barely knew me. He took me under his wing, and he showed me how to be a real man. A nice guy. One that makes good decisions. Or tries to. He was golden. Pure golden. There's a reason that there is nobody else around like Joe. Nobody else could do what he did. I don't even think in the next million years there could be another Joe. He's with the angels now.'

Chapter 6: Mony a mickle maks a muckle!

W hether you knew my Granda in 1968, 1993 or 2015, you will know that he loved a bargain. As per the stories of Joe's international travel, you will by now have reached the conclusion that he thought of himself as a bit of an entrepreneur. My Granda's sales background is a bit like the story of "What came first, the chicken or the egg?" I couldn't pinpoint if it started when he was a kitchen salesman, a political canvasser or a buckie

The voice of reason

picking entrepreneur at the age of eight but I can only imagine that at one point in his life, he thought, "Hey, I'm pretty good at this!" and nobody decided to tell him otherwise.

'It was the summer of '91 and the tall ships had come to Aberdeen. Joe and Neil Christie had organised to buy sailors' hats to sell. They put two plus two together and for once got four: there was going to be a lot of people there celebrating, so why not bring along some souvenirs that could be sold for an inflated price? When the crowds came in to see the ships, they were all over these stupid hats. Joe and Neil made a fortune. Joe had a taste of successful entrepreneurship and so it grew from there.'

June 1992 was the European Championships in Sweden. You might remember that Scotland finished at the top of qualifying group 2 ahead of Switzerland, Romania, Bulgaria, and San Marino with eleven points from eight games. Remembering his success from the year before, when Granda was heading off to Sweden, he decided to make another go of it.

'Joe turned up to the airport with 3 large suitcases.

"Fit's in the cases Joe?" We asked curiously. He unzipped his suitcases to reveal thousands of C U Jimmy hats. Everyone was in stitches. Joe had a rare time trying to navigate three suitcases around the airport. Fucking thousands of them there was. And you didn't expect that he was going to manage them all by himself once he got to Sweden, did you? Oh no, he had us carry them onto a bus on the way and humph them to the game. The bags were ripping, and we were sweating. They became our worst enemy.

But do you know what? He made a fortune selling them too. One of our friends told us that when he was on a separate bus driving up to the game, that he saw hundreds of locals walking about with "those bloody tartan hats on" and he said, "Joe McGunnigle has been here before us!"'

The victims of my Granda's business – They thought they were just going to watch Scotland play!

So, when along came the summer of '97 and the tall ships came back to Aberdeen, Granda bought double the load of sailors' hats that he bought the first time. Only this time, he hardly sold any.

If you ever visited our house in the past twenty years, you would know that there were bags upon bags of sailors' hats (leftover stock), stored in the communal drying room. Granda had turned it into something of a personal warehouse once he'd realized most of the neighbours were too old to climb up the stairs of our building and use the drying room. Me and my Auntie Karen only got rid of them recently because Granda did not allow the mere mention of disposing of the sailors' hats, even though they had been sitting about for twenty years and their value had decreased to virtually nothing. He did make a shot of selling them on eBay but that didn't amount to much. It did however stoke the fire of an unhealthy relationship with the online world.

Ever since Granda completed his 'Computing for Beginners' course in 2009, he loved the internet and all its possibility. This is where he learned his tech skills and was then able to effectively operate M.I.T through a desktop computer in his bedroom. It was good for things such as storing documents and booking flights, but not so good because it opened the black hole into the world wide web.

It started with eBay, but Groupon later came on the scene. Although Granda was unsuccessful in selling his sailors' hats, he realised that he could find success in another department: buying. He bought endless amounts of rubbish and in excessive quantities too. Electric doorbells, teeth whitening kits (despite having no teeth) and Tupperware in every size. You name it, we had it.

But the worst purchase of all had to be a ringing key finder. It was designed as a keyring and if you ever couldn't find your keys, you had to clap three times and they would ring. However, this £1.99 contraption was extremely sensitive and would ring like an alarm almost every few seconds, whether you clapped or not. I think he was just excited by the prospect of eBay, and who could really blame him? Buying tat is exciting but it's even more exciting if it's a bargain.

It wasn't just in the many countries Granda visited that he sold his merchandise, but on his domestic trips too. When you have a busload of fifty guys, there is very little they could do to escape a sales pitch and if you were tactical (which Granda was) and waited until an hour had passed and everybody was drunk, they would buy six of what was being sold!

'Joe was always selling tat on his buses. "Do you want a Scotland mug?" he would ask.

"I'm away to the football, what am I going to do with a coffee mug all day, Joe?" I would laugh. Did I ever buy any of his merchandise? No, did I hell, because I knew Joe and I knew how little it cost

All in good jest

in the first place. Some of these younger boys were easier targets. It was their first game and I always laughed when I could hear them say "Oh brilliant Joe, that's a great deal, I'll take five."'

Something Granda had picked up for a few pounds, he would later sell for a tenner on the way down to Hampden. That was part of the attraction and people would always expect it.

'I did get a nice Scotland top once and for only £10 too. It looked very real, but you didn't ask too many questions!'

As for the £10 Scotland tops, I can't tell you where they came from, but I do recall a bulky stock of various football tops, maybe just enough to

And this was just his personal collection!

fill a large shop (or drying room!)

'I could go on about Joe's flat on Nelson Street. Some of us went there to buy our Scotland tickets. Some of us went there after the pub shut, with the guarantee of a whisky and a Joe special (him entertaining for 7

hours straight) but only some of us knew it for what it really was. A warehouse of tartan bonnets.'

It was often left to me to try and flog some of the great build-up of Granda's buys. Some of you may remember in 2020, I was desperately pushing to sell forty limited edition prints of Hampden. But why have forty in the first place? Why not one, or maybe two if you wanted one up in your toilet too, but forty?! Well as you can guess, they were bought with the intention of reselling, but it just never happened. He just never got round to it.

Me and Granda were notorious for getting round to things. I suspect I inherited this trait from him because he was very good at it and so am I. As you could imagine, when an older man and a teenager live together, certain tasks are forgotten about. Or not forgotten about but at least not prioritised.

Thankfully Auntie Karen came down most days to help out with things and each time we would explain to her that we were "honestly getting round to it." This officially became a joke we shared when I came home from work one day and Granda had a brown envelope waiting for me. "I bought you a gift", he said. I opened it excitedly. I pulled out a bit of card in the shape of a circle, and on it, it read:

"This will help you to get things done. For years you've been saying you'll do things when you get a round tuit. Now you've finally got one!"

Chapter 7: Up to nae good

Let's start by saying that Granda enjoyed a tipple from time to time. He loved celebrating his beloved Scotland – win or lose and there was no better way for him to do it than with a wee Glenmorangie. He once shared to his Facebook page:

'That's me ready for the game. I'm having a pre-match Glenmorangie and a nip for every goal we score. I am going to be slightly inebriated.'

He later commented on the post:
'That's three Glenmorangie's now. Scotland haven't scored three times though. I am just rewinding back to the same first goal over and over again.'

And there was only one thing that Granda enjoyed more than a tipple at home and that was a tipple when travelling the world to see Scotland play. But what comes along with slight alcohol consumption when on holiday with the Tartan Army? I'll tell you. Antics.

'I remember going to the famous 3-2 game in Cyprus with Joe and the late Billy Forsyth. After the game, there was no sign of Joe – nothing unusual there. Suddenly, out of nowhere, we heard 'Flower of Scotland' being belted out. We turned around and there was Joe and Billy, swinging on the back of a tractor, singing their heart out to the national anthem.'

Granda and his dear friend Billy

I can't say much for how Granda's singing was when performing under those conditions, but he really was a great singer. I think many people became acquainted with one of his all-time favourites 'Two little boys', which he often ended up performing at parties and even handed out the lyrics on his buses to Hampden.

And if you haven't heard it. Go and listen to it now before you read on.

"Two little boys had two little toys, each had a wooden horse,

Gaily they played each summer's day, warriors both of course,

One little chap then had a mishap, broke off his horse's head,

Wept for his toy then cried with joy, as his young playmate said,

Did you think I would leave you crying, when there's room on my horse for two,

Climb up here Jack and don't be crying, I can go just as fast with two,

When we grow up, we'll both be soldiers and our horses will not be toys,

And I wonder if we'll remember when we were two little boys.

Long years had passed, war came so fast, bravely they marched away,

Cannon roared loud, and in the mad crowd, wounded and dying lay,

Up goes a shout, a horse dashes out, out from the ranks so blue,
Gallops away to where Joe lay, then came a voice he knew,
Did you think I would leave you dying, when there's room on my horse for two,
Climb up here Joe, we'll soon be flying, I can go just as fast with two."

From a young age when Granda sang me that song I always thought it to be so hauntingly beautiful. It reads such a strong message in which I could see many of Granda's principles, like selflessness and loyalty. The song was even more special because one of the boys was called Joe.

Granda always sang to me as a young girl, and I loved it when he did. He would sit at my bedside and sing, whilst he waited for me to drift off to sleep. One of his other favourite songs to sing was called 'The Special Years' and it still sticks with me to this day.

"Slow up, don't rush to grow up, you'll be a woman before long, so stay a while in the special years, their

magic will soon be gone."

He had a beautiful voice and he always used it at just the right times.

'When we were on the trip to Malta, we were on the bus back from the game and it was a public bus full of Italian school kids. The Tartan Army boys were singing and chanting football songs and in response the Italian children started singing the Italian version of Frère Jacques. Then your Granda stood up on the bus and started singing it with them. He knew every word. He sang it all in Italian. It was like the second coming of Jesus; I don't know how he knew it. It was absolutely hilarious because he was singing with all of these kids, giving it laldy and it was as if he was their teacher. He had a lot of known talents hidden away. I think that was one of his last matches away from home."

Okay, so I thought I would start off with a bit of a 'PG' story about singing with some children. I don't want to continue in a direction that is more or less inaccurate, so let's now shift towards the stories that would give those wee Italian children nightmares.

'We were in Croatia and the hotel we were staying in looked as if it was from the Victorian ages. It had a wooden lift with a chain door – it just looked dodgy. I refused to use it and just took the stairs every time. It was one of Joe's deals of course.

It was the first night and we were all in our beds. At about 4am, I heard Joe's voice outside my room. I decided to ignore it because that's just what Joe did. I thought to myself, "He'll be going round everyone's room seeing who's got any alcohol and who he could keep awake until the birds start singing." So, the next day I saw him at breakfast, he said "Fucking hell, I got in that lift last night and it broke. The doors wouldn't open. I was shouting for help for four hours."

I said, "I heard you, but I just thought you were doing your usual!"

"No, I was stuck in that lift all night until the cleaners started work in the morning! Then they had to winch it down!"

I never used to tell Joe my room number. He would come knocking at 4am saying "Les I know you're

awake" and if you let him in, he'd be there for hours. Which is reasonable at any other time of the day but not at four in the morning. I would be

Always on the wind up

like "Joe, I've heard all your stories, in fact I was in 75% of your fucking stories". I joke about it now but what I would give to have him sitting on the end of my bed once more speaking his famous shite."

To be honest, any chance to speak (or sing) would suit Granda perfectly, whether it was by my bedside or to a crowd of people but arm him with a megaphone and you're in for some performance. Well, excluding the time I saw him get electrocuted and fall to the ground after using one. Perhaps that should have been a warning.

'We landed in Tokyo airport a bit worse for wear thanks to the free drinks on the plane. Something Joe

was partial towards. We went to the bus terminal, which was enormous; bearing in mind it was part of a major international airport. Joe walked up to a little Japanese gentleman that was doing the bus announcements and asked:

"Which bus do we get to our hotel in Tokyo?"

The little man looked very confused. It might have had something to do with the Japanese accent that Joe was attempting.

Next, Joe started pointing at the megaphone that the gentleman was holding, which just made him even more confused. Joe continued pointing at the megaphone and then pointed at himself... So, the daft wee man handed it over to Joe and without hesitation he proceeded to sing at the top of his lungs, "TOKYO, TOKYO, WE ARE THE FAMOUS TARTAN ARMY AND WE ARE HERE IN TOKYO" twice over, which we all joined in with. The little man went absolutely crazy and grabbed it from Joe and we had the entire airport staring at us, wondering what the hell they just heard. Your Granda had a way of smoothing situations over like that and thankfully we got away from the airport without being arrested.'

Granda enjoyed a bit of airport banter. Even more so when it was in Aberdeen because it was always the starting point of the journey. Every Scotland fan so excited and full of zest and hope for the game that was yet to happen. Aberdeen Airport was the pre-match warm up. To Granda, there was nowhere he would rather have been than sipping an ice-cold beer at 6am on a Monday morning. Well actually, there is one place he might have rather been and that was the Duty-Free shop when they were handing out Whisky samples!

'At Aberdeen airport, we were all waiting for our flight to Iceland and duty-free were giving out free samples of a whisky. Mostly everyone refused because it was so early in the morning but not Joe. In fact, I think Joe made up for everyone else's refusal of the whisky samples by drinking for them. When we were on the aircraft, a police officer appeared at the front of the plane and approached our group and asked the cabin crew and Joe if he was okay for boarding. Thankfully Joe managed to muster together something that made the officer believe him and then he nodded off to sleep and didn't wake up until touchdown!'

So, boozing at the airport is great. Free samples at the airport are also great. But not when you have responsibilities. I can't begin to imagine the stress it must have caused Granda, to have managed a group of forty guys. Although, I think given his extensive experience in drunk people management, he was an expert in the field. And, as it turns out, there are much worse things you can do when you are responsible for a group of people!

'We were over in Kiev to play Ukraine. The day we arrived, we took a tour of the Chernobyl Reactor and Pripyat. None of us wanted to go to begin with but Joe convinced us otherwise. It turned out to be one of the most memorable things I have ever done. That was something that could only have happened following Scotland and even more so being on one of Joe's trips. He always made time for tourism and culture.

After the tour, the guide took us to the army barracks of the old Soviet army and they served us purple soup for lunch, which I thought was strange enough but then they brought out lots of bottles of vodka. It was clearly homemade and had no labels. So, I guess our tour became a party! Again, something that could only happen with Joe.

We all had a shot just to play along but then we had another and then another and then another. Most folk said no more at that point. The tour guide said that you could only stop on an even number of shots, so we had some more. I remember your Granda nudging the person next to him and pointing over to someone.... The bus driver of the tour was matching everyone else shot for shot on what must have been lethal 100% homemade vodka. It was then Joe turned around and looked at us with a dreaded expression and said, "This guy's got to drive us home."'

When Granda travelled to various countries, he didn't just go for the football: he fully immersed himself in the country and always made the most of his time there. He would do his best to blend in with the locals and take part in their traditions and celebrations. When he was in impoverished countries, he wouldn't hesitate to offer conversation to people and take the time to learn about their livelihood. And in a similar sense, when he was in prosperous and wealthy countries, he would without a doubt try and channel his chameleon abilities. But as the saying definitely does not go: You can take the boy out of Woodside, but you can't take the Woodside out of the boy!

'There seemed to be a few years where we kept getting drawn against Slovenia, Slovakia, Lithuania, Moldova - those kind of shite European teams that were in the same category as us. You know, plum; they were in the plum category. Even against them, we still couldn't win! My Dad went over to watch Scotland against Estonia and the game got called off because Estonia never turned up. He went all the way over there, the Scotland team were standing on the pitch, ready to start and the referee blew his whistle, but nobody came.

So of course, he decided to write in to "Captain Cash" at the Daily Record. Captain Cash was like an Agony Aunt that provided financial support to people that had been scammed. He gave him a sob story about how he was the Tartan Army foot soldier general that went all the way over to Estonia and the game was postponed. He explained to Captain Cash that he had spent all his money on the Estonia trip and that he now had no money to go to the return game which was going to be held in Monaco. And you can bet your bottom dollar that Captain Cash not only funded his flights and hotel to Monaco but two tickets to the game, too. Monte Carlo, Monaco.

I think he had to choose wisely who he asked. So must have thought,
"Right fa can I take with me that's got a couple of quid."
So, I got the phone call.
"Aye son, you ken you're my favourite."
I said:
"Right Da, what you wanting?"
"I've got two tickets to go to Monaco. There's nobody else I'd rather take with me."
I had a wee lump in my throat.
I said, "Right Dad, when we going?"
My wife in the background was shouting, "you're nae going awa imorn!".
I said, "I've got to go with my Dad, I'm nae letting him go to Monaco by himself."

So right enough, the very next day, me and my Dad headed off to Monaco.

Now, this was Monte Carlo I'm talking about, so we had our finest clothes on. My Dad was wearing a white suit and really looked the part. There were a few other of the boys that had travelled over for the game too and so we met up with them to head into a casino that was in the heart of Monte Carlo.

Before we went in, my Dad said to us, "Right listen boys, naebody kens us here. I need you to pretend to be my bodyguards."

We all had black suits and ties on and my Dad was shining like the tooth fairy in his white get up. I think it was me, Paul Bonner and Stuart Forbes. He said, "Right guys, you have all got black on and I've got on white on so I'm going to be the person that's very important. Now don't look at me, just stand at either side of me and look straight ahead."

So that was us, we walked into the biggest casino in Monte Carlo, up the red carpeted stairs, the three of us walking alongside him, looking for any danger coming, like we were protecting Rod Stewart. People were in awe. They wondered who this pop star could possibly be. A Scottish music mogul? A member of the royal family? Wait, could it have actually been Rod Stewart? We finally got inside the place and my Dad had about eight quid. And I thought I was flush with only 20!'

But you could be assured that even with eight pounds Granda could have charmed the socks off every person in that place. Money can go so far in a casino but when you run out of it there's not much else you can do. Personality on the other hand is a timeless accomplice that will keep you there, or anywhere for that matter.

'Something your Granda would do if he was walking up George Street, He would see people leaving a party, walking out of the front door saying, "See you later Fred, thanks for the party" and your Granda would go right up to that party. Somebody would say to him. "Who are you with?" He would say, "Oh, I'm with Fred!" because he heard the guy's name outside, and I kid you not, he would well and truly convince Fred himself that he had known him for years. That's

the kind of thing he would do. He was so quick off the mark it was unreal.'

Even if people didn't know Granda, they would quickly get to know him, and he would become the most interesting person at the party. If I could make up the best possible party attendee, it would be him! In Aberdeen and across the globe he started to gain a reputation as the man with the tartan jacket, the crazy Scotsman. People he met across the pond always kept in contact with him and were so keen to meet up when he would inevitably return to those countries. In fact, sometimes he was so ahead of the game that he would speak with football fans from across the world and arrange to meet them abroad before he even got there. Who knows how he found them in the first place. Perhaps they saw him on Mexican TV!

'Joe had been in contact with some Japanese guy years before this trip, who happened to support Dundee. When the guy found out the Tartan Army were coming to Japan, he insisted on meeting up with Joe and giving him a tour of Tokyo. It was so generous because the guy worked six days a week and had only

one day off and he chose to spend it with us. That was special.'

I think it's fair to say that a tour guide in Tokyo may have been somewhat beneficial. One thing that Granda was notorious for was wandering off, never to be seen again. Whether he was at the other side of the world or at a match in Hampden, you could be certain that the "Joe disappearing act" would happen. But naturally, if you were the organizer of the trip, you could disobey your own rules. If you wanted to disappear, sure, disappear to your heart's content, but if anyone else wanted to pull the same trick, it was just not on.

'My favourite memory was the frequent reminder to be back at the bus for the 10.30pm departure for a midweek Hampden game. It was quite the task to get out of the game once the final whistle blew at 9.45pm, get a sausage supper carry out before 10pm curfew, and then onto the bus by Joe's strict cut-off time.

Regular as clockwork though, there would be no sign of Joe as 10.30 pm passed and he would end up being the only foot soldier posted missing. Following numerous phone calls and search parties, he would eventually stumble onto the bus closer to 11pm, without a care in the world and start to tap up everyone for a drink and feed.'

'I remember on many occasions being the one to have to go find Joe as he was always late back on the bus and would have to dig him out of The Montford after games, usually at the cost of a Glenmorangie.'

But Granda disappearing locally in the likes of Glasgow wasn't too difficult to overcome. He could often be found in all the usual haunts. It was disappearing in foreign countries where nobody spoke English and there could have been a potential risk of him being in danger, abducted or worse, being AWOL with everyone's match tickets in his pocket, that was the real problem.

'When we were in Poland, I well and truly lost Joe. We were in a pub, speaking to a couple of fans and I turned around and he had disappeared. I didn't see him until the next day. I said where have you been Joe?

He had been wandering about the streets and stumbled across a marble building with a big red carpet outside. Polish royalties were getting married. There were some guests there who were high up in governance and from the Polish Establishment. Joe spent the whole night at the royal wedding. He got past the security guard and everything and somehow strolled in with his kilt on and enjoyed the lavish party all night!'

That's the difficult thing about being a people person, one thing leads to another, one person leads to a royal wedding ceremony and Bob's your uncle, yet another disappearing act has occurred.

'My Dad got us tickets for the Champions League final in Ireland. Scotland weren't playing in it, but he had been gifted them through his associations with the S.A.F.A. When we arrived in Dublin, we got a taxi into the city. It was absolutely mobbed. It just so happened that the queen was doing a visit there for the very first time. The streets were all coming to a standstill, and we couldn't get to our hotel. The roads were blocked off and there were snipers on every roof.

So next thing, I look round. He's gone. Ken when the next time I saw him was? On the plane going home. I swear to God. I said, "Where the hell have you been?" And out he came with it, the famous... "Ahh. That would be telling!"

He said "Dublin... it's good though is it".

I said "Aye fit wandering aboot yourself? Nae really!"'

Sometimes Granda got intentionally lost and sometimes he got unintentionally lost and there is a difference. No matter what though, he could always rely on his buddies to find him and solve the problem.

'We were in Paris; it was the night that McFadden scored when we won 1-0. Now Paris is a big place. Some other guys and I got lost trying to get back to our hotel. We said, "Right, we need to flag down a taxi, we're not walking any further."

We waved at a couple, but they weren't stopping. Finally, one pulled into the side of the road and who else was sitting in the passenger seat other than Joe himself. He said,

"Where are you boys going?" I told him that we were going to our hotel. "Just get in the back", Joe said.

So, the three of us got in his taxi, and we more or less went round the corner and we arrived at Joe's hotel. He stopped the driver and said to him,

"You take these boys to their hotel."

We said to Joe, "Cheers Joe we'll get your fare when we pay, thanks for stopping for us. The driver went round another corner and there was our hotel. We would have been quicker walking. We got out of the taxi, and the driver charged us 53 euros. "What?!" I said.

The driver said, "That man.. He had been in the taxi for a long time."

The next day I saw Joe and I said to him, "Hey min, you're owe me 53 euros for that!"

He said, "I did think I had been in the taxi for a wee while. I got lost too!"

Whether he was really lost or just on the wind-up, we'll never know. Although Granda could disappear like smoke, his regular and inimitable presence in the local news always ensured that those around him and back at home, knew exactly what he was up to when following the Tartan Army. The one downside of being a local media star!

'We were in Japan; it was the day after the game and Joe was on the phone to your Nana from a phone box. Cath said to him,

"Aye, you've started smoking again!"

He had been stopped for a few years at this point. Joe turned around and said, "Fucking Japanese technology... She must be able to smell my breath through the phone!"

Cath shouted down the phone, "No Joe, you and Les are on the front page of the Daily Record and you've got a fag hanging out of your mouth!!"'

Granda didn't get up to anything out of the ordinary. He just tended to meet new people and enjoy himself whilst on "duty". I believe as he got older, he started to ca'canny a bit...

He gave Billy Connolly a run for his money!

Do I believe that? No! Do you? No. And that was what we loved about him the most. Even in his seventies he still had his sharp tongue, incredible humour, and devilish charm. Granda's qualities were timeless and as he grew older, they stayed exactly as they were. Do I think he would have looked back and regretted anything in his life? Not a single bit. Not a single ounce of it. I think he would have looked back and been proud of how he dealt with every single situation that he encountered – with humility and hilarity. With the Joe McGunnigle magic.

'Six of us were travelling down to Wembley in a Volkswagen campervan. Joe was the responsible driver. We were on the road and were all enjoying a drink in the back seats. We had been driving for a few hours when Graeme Sangster said,
"Joe, I'll take a shot at driving."
"Aye, ok", your Granda said.
At that time, you drunk and drove anyway. Anything went. I don't even think we had licenses. So, Graeme is now driving and your Granda's having a beer. I think we had all fallen asleep and we woke up to your Granda saying, "Graeme, far ye gan min?".
Graeme had gone the whole way round the roundabout at Perth and we were now back in Stonehaven! We had lost about 5 hours of our journey.

So back in the right direction we went, stopping at various stops on the way in different parts of England. We got to a place called Ganton and noticed that the vehicle was making strange noises. A couple of "trchkkkk, trchkkk, trchkkk's" later, we broke down. As if the trip couldn't get any worse. Your Granda took it into the nearest garage, and it was about £300 for a new clutch that would take two days to fix. We were going to have to leave it and hire a car.

Your Granda came out of the garage with the guy that worked there and was being shown a Cortina that was for hire. When the guy saw there were six of us, he said that there was no way he would hire it out – the Cortina only held four. So, Joe told two of the boys to hide in the bushes and you better believe we hired the Cortina. We picked up the other two round the corner and now had four of us in the back. Fuck's sake.

Finally, we were just about at Wembley and in front of our car driving up Wembley Way was the England Team bus. Peter Shilton who was the English goalkeeper (I'll never forget this), was looking out the back of the bus, with a couple of players and your

Granda and his brother Frank, in the front, and I swear I could lipread him saying "Look at these idiots". He had all the English team looking in and laughing at us.

I can't tell you much more than that other than by the end of it we were bleezing and skint. After the game, we drove the Cortina back to the Garage to pay for the work that had

Granda and friends at Wembley

been done with the clutch and swapped the cars over.

We were now driving homeward bound in our camper van when the car conked out of petrol. Joe turned around to Blackie and said,
"Blackie, where's that twenty quid I gave you to hold on to for petrol?"
Blackie revealed that he had spent the last penny they had on beer.

Your Granda was going nuts at Blackie and Glasgow Peter was in the back of the van smoking a joint and laughing his heed off.

Joe turned around and looked us dead in the eye.

"We're going to have to siphon petrol," he said. "Does anyone have a hacksaw?"

Peter burst out laughing and said "Aye, because we normally bring a hacksaw to Wembley."

It was now 3am but we managed to get hold of a tube and started to siphon a few cars. I think we managed to get half a tank. We almost got to Edinburgh and the car started running out of petrol again. Your Granda decided, "We canna do this anymore."

He pulled into a garage, cleared his throat, and headed inside. Preparing to do a "Joe special".

He told the worker, "I'm so sorry, we used all our money to get our car fixed, is there any chance I could fill my car up and I could send you a cheque when I get back to Aberdeen? We've got nothing left but take me for my word I will send a cheque down if you could fill up the van. And the guy did it. And we got hame. We hadn't had a wash for about three days and we stunk of petrol. But if anyone else had of went in and asked for that free fill up, we would have been told to fuck off. And right as rain, Joe sent the cheque back, the very next day. Because Joe McGunnigle was always a man of his word.'

Chapter 8: The cycle back home

When I was born, my Granda was 55. He was very much still in full speed of life at that stage. But in those later years, as I grew older, and he grew older too, he kept the same momentum. He moved forward with the same energy and the same spark. I admired that so much.

Granda was the football man. He was the guy that organised the Scotland trips, he was the amateur football guy, the guy with the great team. The guy that everybody knew. But aside from that, first and foremost, he was the family man. A family man like no other. He loved love. He loved to hold his dear ones close, he loved to hug, he loved to smile and make special memories. And he loved recounting memories and reminiscing, talking about times that were good. Times that were simple.

Somebody once said to me that when Nana died, Granda lost his sparkle. I'm not sure I ever liked the comparison, but I understood it. I was only eleven when my Nana died, and I didn't really understand her death. I always thought that if I prayed, she would get better. But she didn't. I watched the man I loved the most, lose the person he loved the most and it was unbearable at times. The person who was my rock, I would watch lock himself in his room and break down into tears. The person who I relied on for being strong and unbreakable was shown to be breakable. And I suppose that is where I started to understand life.

I remember the day Nana died, I painted a picture of me and Granda holding hands. When I was painting it, I remember being confused about what more I could do and if painting a picture was really going to help anyone at all. I gave it  to him, and I told him it was me and him against the world. And from then on it was.

There was some speculation after my Nana died whether I would go and live elsewhere but that was just as confusing for me to hear as it was to Granda.

Me and Granda at my 21st party

Me and Granda, against the world. We couldn't do that without each other, could we? And we did it. It wasn't the most conventional family photograph and at times as individuals we struggled, but together, me and Granda were unbreakable. We needed each other more than ever in the years to follow that. We got through them thanks to our amazing family and friends. We made so much more of those special memories that Granda loved. We cried, we laughed, and we continued to love, and we always took the time to speak about the wonderful woman that was my Nana.

My beautiful Nana

Granda's later life, as most will know, was somewhat tainted by a cancer diagnosis. He was diagnosed in 2017 with a rare stage four head and neck cancer and even with a prognosis so grim, he managed to chuckle at the doctors and say "A rare cancer? *Well, I am a rare specimen.*"

Granda was to have an operation to remove what they could of the tumour. He was told that even with the operation the cancer wouldn't really ever go away but it could prolong his life. The surgery was huge. It took around 18 hours and involved getting his neck cut open and most of his tongue being removed and being reconstructed with a skin graft from his arm. There was a possibility that he would never speak again, and it was a guarantee that he would never be able to taste or eat again like he had ever before.

I will always remember the night before Granda had to go into hospital to have his teeth removed in preparation for surgery later that week. We had an Ashvale, as a sort of "last supper". We ate our Ashvale with my Auntie Karen and we laughed about normal things, even though our minds were far from being normal. Granda had been diagnosed with terminal cancer and on that night, he was laughing about the fact that I could hold a mug in between my toes. I don't know what the reality was for him but to me, he was just being Granda.

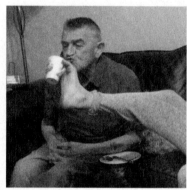

Granda was fairly humoured by my skill

I do not want to end this book by focusing on my Granda's diagnosis itself because it far from defines him. But the way he tackled his cancer has changed the way me and many others look at life. Saying "tackled" alone would have been a no from him. He did not see himself as a "warrior" or "of great bravery". I certainly saw those things, but to him, he was just living.
"You just have to carry on," he would say.
"What other choice have I got?"

He didn't enjoy spending time in hospital, but he didn't dwell on it. My Granda developed a great camaraderie with the nurses, doctors, and patients that were there too. He was always winding up the staff and loved making silly videos and photos to share on his Facebook page whilst he was in hospital. At one point, he made me produce a film, with him as the main star, trying to discourage people in the hospital from using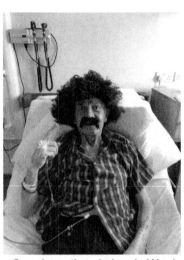

Granda on the wind-up in Ward 114

hospital TV and to buy a Samsung tablet instead for £20 a month (it even came with internet), and no, he wasn't on commission from Samsung. The nurses lapped him up. He was forever flirting with them and making them laugh until they looked as if they would cry. I can't begin to imagine how difficult it must be for the staff who care for people with cancer but to have someone like my Granda kept their spirits high.

My Granda loved everyone being together. He loved

celebrating with people and so it seemed apt that for his 75th birthday we threw him a huge party. Auntie Karen took charge of catering, and I was responsible for sending out invites and party organisation. It was a massive gathering which was well over the venue capacity. There were old and new friends from afar, family and people that he hadn't connected

Me, Granda and Karen at his 75th

with for years. My Granda had the night of his life. This was the year before he got very ill, and I've always been so glad that we managed to give him the huge celebration that he really wanted. It was a night that we all still remember so fondly. What a party.

But there was no other time in my Granda's life where he was the star of the show quite like when he took part in BRAVE.

It was January 2018 and we were in Aberdeen Airport

before heading off on holiday to Tenerife. My Auntie Karen had planned for us to go away to enjoy some sun after my Granda had recently finished another round of gruelling chemotherapy. She had managed to swindle us into the V.I.P lounge and my Granda was sitting enjoying a single vodka (after being told by Karen that he couldn't have a double), when his phone rang. He answered.

"Hello. Hello, yes this is Joe, who is this?"

He screwed his face up and turned around to us.

"Karen, I don't know who this is, it's someone going on about modelling, they might have the wrong–", Karen grabbed the phone from him and bounced out of the room.

When she returned, she was absolutely beaming. Her grin was as wide as a Cheshire Cat's. Equally as confused as each other, me and Granda awaited an explanation.

"Dad, you're going to be a model!"

Granda had an expression that was somewhat surprised, but also not completely flabbergasted by the idea that Karen may have just had a lucrative offer from Chanel or Gucci on his behalf.

"You're going to be a BRAVE model this year!"

Still making little sense to us, Karen elaborated. She explained that she had read that Friends of Anchor were looking for 24 male models that had experienced or were currently facing a cancer diagnosis. The deadline had been the day previous, and Karen with only one hour to apply, sent one in. And my Granda only went and got picked.

Granda getting in the practice on holiday after the news

Friends of Anchor are a charity based in the North-East of Scotland that exist to make the difference in cancer treatment and support services. I had heard of Courage on the Catwalk before, which is their annual female catwalk, but I was not aware that, the year before my Granda was picked, Friends of Anchor organised their first show for men, "BRAVE". The idea of the event is to raise vital funds for the charity but also to empower men and give them an experience that is so far removed from that of cancer treatment and time spent in hospital.

The lead up to the event was so busy. My Granda spent a lot of time fundraising, gaining sponsorship and raising awareness about what he was doing. He had to attend weekly model training sessions, organised by Friends of Anchor and a professional local modelling agency 'Premier Productions' who kindly donated their time and services. He had pre-event photo shoots (some of you may remember his flagship photo with his own chosen quote), newspaper

Granda getting fitted in his Hugo Boss suit

interviews, professional fittings at John Lewis and Gibbs Menswear. During all which he was still receiving chemotherapy, where he would often stay in hospital for a week at a time.

I still to this day struggle to comprehend the incredible fate of my Auntie Karen seeing the application deadline for the event and putting Granda forward for it with only 24 hours left. If there was something he was born to do, it was that, and if there was ever a time that we needed it most, it was then. Despite dealing with his own diagnosis and the struggles that came with it, BRAVE gave us all something special as a family. I wouldn't say it

Granda's chosen quote: "Haud Gaun" – Scottish Doric for "Keep Going"

distracted us from the reality of what Granda was facing, but it shifted the focus to something positive. We were celebrating his bravery. BRAVE gave us a reason to, every day.

BRAVE was a home away from home for Granda. The twenty-three other guys who took part were of all different ages and walks of life, but it didn't take long before they became "BRAVE brothers". I felt just as proud watching all of them perform when the night finally arrived because we quickly got to know the other models and their families and there was an incredible comfort in all being there to support a loved one for the same reason.

When May 11th came, we were all a mixed bag of emotions. My Granda had only been out of hospital for a few days and was quite weak. We were worried about his ability to walk on stage. But in true Joe McGunnigle fashion, *nothing*, not even chemotherapy, was going to debilitate him and stop him from strutting his stuff.

The event was held at The Aberdeen Beach Ballroom; it was unbelievably glamorous. The sell-out event had hundreds in attendance and our family were lucky enough to have a table by the front. The evening started with some speeches from the FoA team and videos that were shown of the models' background stories.

When the lights hit centre stage and the models came out for their first walk of the night, we lost all inhibitions. We were screaming so wildly; if the stage, lights and crowd disappeared, it could have seemed from pain or fear. But it was pride, it was love. Our hero, our incredibly brave, handsome, most beloved hero was on the stage, dressed to the nines – and it looked as if he had been modelling his entire life. He was grooving, he was dancing, he was working the whole crowd and when it was his time to do a solo walk down the front of the catwalk, everyone just *lost their shit*. My Granda had secretly snuck a bunch of roses down the front of his trousers; he was dancing to an Elvis Presley track, with golden sunglasses on, and he was whipping pink roses out of his pants and throwing them to the crowd. His performance was astronomical. I have never in my life been so proud of any person than I was of my Granda that night.

But the truth is, I've always looked up to my Granda. I've always naturally believed in him because he was wise, and he was caring and considerate of other people and that is the kind of person we all need to look up to. But nothing compares to how much he inspired me in how he tackled his cancer diagnosis. He was dignified, and even when we

Granda ROCKING the catwalk

were scared, he was fearless. He showed continual resilience during what was probably the scariest time of his life. How can I fear anything in life when that was the man, *the superhero*, that raised me? But to him, he was none of those things. He was just Joe. The guy that bloody loved following Scotland, wearing his trademark tartan jacket.

My superhero

Joe's famous tartan jacket is now on display in Hampden Football stadium. A fitting tribute to a piece of history. He donated his jacket to the museum once before but then realised it was far

The General and his soldiers

too iconic to be there whilst he was alive and so he took

it back. A Scotland game was not a Scotland game if you didn't see Joe McGunnigle and his technicolour team coat.

Many people would recognize that jacket before they recognized my Granda. It was known all over the world.

Me and Auntie Karen with Granda's jacket

My Auntie Karen and I went down to visit the jacket on display and were given a tour of the museum. It was a truly special day, filled with mixed emotions but mostly pride. The display is a true honour to my Granda. In a beautiful lit up memorial, his jacket shines in all its glory.

A fitting tribute for Hampden's own

A single jacket that holds a thousand memories.

A jacket that took him near and far, now resting in the place he called home. The place where the journey all began, his cycle to Hampden.

That initial journey to Hampden, McGunnigle International and Domestic Travel, the people my Granda met when following Scotland, his dearest friends from his hometown, his hustling and bustling, the games he lived by, the pain of watching opportunities slip through the fingers of his beloved team, the late nights, the early mornings, the planning, the dedication, were all parts of his life. Small, meaningful parts that made up the sum of the man he was and continues to be remembered by. Parts of his life that are now told through story or shared over a dram. And so, my job here is done. I made it *my duty* to bring these stories together, so they make sense as a whole. Just like the badges on my Granda's jacket.

His jacket wouldn't be such a novelty if it only had one badge sewn on to the collar. It's special to people because of just how many there are. It's poignant in that it represents a singular life well lived. Lived like no other.

I hope my Granda's journey meant something to you in some small way. I hope you have read these stories and smiled. Because that's what he would want; to make us smile. That's all he ever wanted.

I believe that we are all on our own cycle to Hampden. Some of us have been there and already returned, whilst some of us are just waiting for the right time to take off.

But we are only ever that one decision away from fulfilling the rest of our lives.

So, whatever it is you want to do, what are you waiting for? Joe McGunnigle didn't wait for a clearer sky, a smoother road or "next time" before he made that special journey.

And neither should you.

It might not be easy.

But you just have to haud gaun.

THE END

In loving memory of Joe and Cath McGunnigle.